Painting Wargaming Figures

Painting Wargaming Figures

Javier Gomez Valero
"El Mercenario"

Pen & Sword
MILITARY

First published in Great Britain in 2015
And reprinted in 2016, 2017 and 2018 by
Pᴇɴ & Sᴡᴏʀᴅ Mɪʟɪᴛᴀʀʏ
an imprint of
Pen & Sword Books Ltd,
47 Church Street,
Barnsley,
South Yorkshire.
S70 2AS

A CIP record for this book is available from the British Library.

ISBN 9781848848221

Printed and bound in India by Replika Press Pvt. Ltd.

Pen & Sword Books Ltd incorporates the Imprints of Pen & Sword Family History,
Pen & Sword Aviation, Pen & Sword Maritime, Pen & Sword Military, Pen & Sword Atlas,
Pen & Sword Discovery, Pen & Sword Politics, Pen & Sword Archaeology, Leo Cooper,
Wharncliffe Local History, Wharncliffe True Crime, Wharncliffe Transport,
Pen & Sword Select, Pen & Sword Military Classics, The Praetorian Press,
Claymore Press, Remember When, Seaforth Publishing and Frontline Publishing

For a complete list of Pen & Sword titles please contact
Pen & Sword Books Limited
47 Church Street, Barnsley, South Yorkshire, S70 2AS, England
E-mail: enquiries@pen-and-sword.co.uk
Website: www.pen-and-sword.co.uk

Contents

Dedication

To my Dad, the real artist of the family and light years ahead of me as a painter.

Preface

A malformed lump of highly toxic lead could hardly be called a beautiful miniature, but it was my first and first times are supposed to be something nice to remember. It was back in the late 1980s that I lost my (painter's) virginity to that Dungeons & Dragons© half-orc, which I stole from my elder brother's collection. I had a great time 'colouring' it with his smelly Humbrol enamels, at least until he caught me and kicked my arse. Anyway, I guess it was worth the effort as I haven't stopped painting miniatures since.

I can't say that I was alien to painting as my father was a draftsman and a painter himself, so that seed germinated easily in me. Like most painters who started this hobby as kids, I began with fantasy figures for my role-playing games (yes, everyone has an obscure past, even me!). One thing led to another and I found myself fascinated by the *Warhammer* world. It helped that my brother opened a local hobby shop (that later became Atlantica Juegos, one of the biggest hobby stores in Europe). However, a good Samaritan (someone desperate and lonely enough to teach a teenager how to play *Empire*) rescued me from the Dark Side and introduced me to historical wargaming. *Napoleonic Empire* came first, then *Ancient Empire* and finally Second World War *Command Decision*. I always liked to learn the hard way!

By seventeen I was quite an experienced wargamer and I started to paint commissions. A couple of years later I joined with my friend and painting colleague David Gomez (although we were not related at all, besides our common last name, some people started to call us the Gomez Brothers) and founded El Mercenario painting service. I learnt a lot from him. David's background was painting bigger scale figures and plastic kits, and we incorporated some of his techniques to our painting style. Shortly afterwards, we won some painting prizes at Salute and other shows and started to work for several companies, especially Perry Miniatures. Moreover, we took the reins of the Spanish magazine *Wargames, Soldiers & Strategy*. I managed the magazine for a couple of years, while David took charge of the painting articles. Later, we swapped roles and I contributed articles and photographs from my own collections. Those were happy days … we lived and breathed for the hobby.

Over time David replaced his worn-out rocker leather jacket for a suit and became a respected gentleman with a proper job. Corporate suits were not made for me: aside from a few years working part-time at my brother's store,

I never had a proper boss. So I decided to keep running El Mercenario by myself. These years as a full-time painter were intense – very intense – painting ten to twelve hours a day, six or seven days a week. I always enjoyed planning new projects, reading about the period to research it and motivate myself properly, looking for the figures, designing the units and then the divisions or the armies and finally painting them. But I never was a collector. Once complete, I sold most of my personal collections. Being a professional painter allowed me to do what I loved and be paid for it! That doesn't mean I stopped doing things for myself, but that is a perilous path for a pro. Like relationships, it would be tempting to cheat on your usual partner and devote more and more time to a new and exciting affair, but hobby affairs don't usually last, and by the end of the month … you have to pay your bills!

Four years ago my life changed deeply. Although I still enjoyed the painting, I felt that I needed something else in my life, and I worked with two friends to publish a new military history magazine called *Desperta Ferro*. The magazine was a complete success; the business expanded very fast but also became more and more demanding. As a day has only twenty-four hours I had to decide between publishing and professional painting, and I chose *Desperta Ferro*, to which I devote my full time, soul and mind. However, I would never quit painting: for me it's much more than a hobby or a job, it's a huge part of my life. My poor old eyes still can see, but in the end my brushes will need to be pried from my cold, dead hands.

Introduction

Before getting down to business I would like to say a few things about my painting technique. First of all, we are not painting 90mm figures destined to be neatly placed in a display cabinet; these are wargame figures intended to build armies from and play games with, so in my opinion the goal is to get the best quality/time investment ratio possible. Although there are several wargame figure sizes, from 40mm to 6mm, this book pays special attention to 28mm miniatures. Many wargamers prefer to play with smaller scales but from a painter's point of view 28mm, given its size and detail, allows me to show all the techniques needed to paint figures, and it's also the size of miniatures I enjoy painting the most. However, the techniques used can be adapted to other scales.

In the past I was accused by purists of doing a rough paint job, with sudden transitions between different highlights and brusque contrasts. Well, sometimes they were right and my painting style has evolved over the years, but my painting goal remains the same: these are not figures (only) to be displayed in a cabinet but to be seen on a wargame table at a certain distance, forming part of bigger units. So, although I always try to paint as realistically as possible, I use strong and vivid colours for my armies.

Regarding my technique, I normally paint a base colour and two highlights (sometimes three for bigger surfaces) over a black-primed figure, a system that became more or less standard in recent years. Ever since Wargames Foundry released their three-shades colour system of paints, where one blister pack contains the base colour, first highlight and second highlight for a certain colour, with no need to mix, many painters made their lives easier and embraced this new concept. I recognize that this has its advantages, especially for painters of huge armies or people with a limited time whose priority is speed, but I still like to mix my own paints. Call me a romantic, but I honestly think that painting is much more than giving accurate brushstrokes. It's all about colours: to choose the proper colours, to mix them to a correct shade, to add different paints to obtain highlight effects. At the risk of sounding old-fashioned, I still prefer the old way rather than the faster, standardized new system of three-shade packaging.

PART ONE
B A S I C S

1

What Do I Need?

PAINTS

The first thing you'll need is some paint (Figure 1). There is quite a wide choice when it comes to water- and solvent-based paints (known respectively as acrylics and enamels), but I highly recommend acrylic paints as they are water-soluble. Even though enamel paints give better coverage, acrylics are easier to use and give your figures a more realistic finish. And a big plus with acrylics is that you can avoid any rows that might arise at home because of the awful smell of enamels. Here are the market's top manufacturers of acrylic paints:

Vallejo: This excellent Spanish brand is world-renowned and offers an indispensable range for any experienced painter. Vallejo offers high-quality paints that cover any surface easily, even when diluted. In general, their paints tend to dry to a matt finish. Vallejo makes up around 90% of my collection of paints and most of those I use on a regular basis. They have several ranges designed for miniatures, airbrushes, fine art and so on. Most of the Vallejos I use are from their Model Color range, a

(Figure 1)

selection of 220 different colours where we can find practically all of the shades we'll need (all coded with a 70 followed by three digits: 800 and above; when I'm describing Vallejo paints elsewhere in this book, I just use these last three numbers for reference). However, I also use some paints from their Arte Deco range (codes from 001 to 150) for two reasons: they are mostly the same colours but are sold in larger 60ml bottles (a good choice to save money in the case of the most frequently used colours, such as Black and White) and they also offer interesting shades like Raw Sienna (113) and Midnight Blue (070).

Andrea: This brand's catalogue has fewer colours than Vallejo's and their paints are not as easy to use. They generally don't cover as well and must be applied very thickly, practically without being diluted at all. Their main advantage, however, is their extra-matt finish. As a fan of matt finishes, sometimes I use Andrea colours such as black, dark blue and different shades of brown when the Vallejo equivalent is too glossy. I often use a mixed combination of Andrea and Vallejo paints: the resulting mixtures cover well and dry to a matt finish.

Games Workshop: This company offers a range focused on painting fantasy miniatures; regardless of this, they are still suitable for use on historical figures. Games Workshop has an average-sized range of paints and they generally give good coverage. Their shades, however, tend to be a bit extravagant and their finishes are often glossy. On the other hand, their range of metallic colours is outstanding and is superior to any other acrylic range I know of.

Undercoat spray

Putting an undercoat on figures before you paint them is extremely important. This helps later paint layers to cover the figure more easily and prevents your masterpiece from chipping once dry. I strongly recommend the use of sprays to prime miniatures for several reasons: it's faster, the coating is thinner than paint you brush on, it dries quickly and the paint is enamel instead of acrylic (so it adheres better over any surface and is stronger and more durable). As we'll see later, the colour used for priming (usually black or white) will determine what painting style we use over it. If we decide to use white as an undercoat, a single layer would be enough, as that will be completely painted over at a later stage, leaving no visible part of the original undercoat. However, if we opt for a black undercoat we would need to touch up the figure with black paint over the spray layer as we have to be sure that even the most hidden parts (especially those!) remain black, because some of this undercoat will remain visible when the figure is finished. Making sure a black undercoated figure is fully covered is especially important for metal figures, as they have more depth than plastic ones; believe me, it's very distressing to find parts where the metal can still be seen when you're half way through painting a figure!

Like any other spray, you must shake the can well before using it. When applying the spray, 'fire' short bursts from about 30cm away from the figure. You always need to hold the can upright rather than upside down because that makes the nozzle clog up and begin to drip. The smell of the propellant given off by sprays is very strong, so always use them in a well-ventilated working area (balcony, terrace or out the window).

There are many undercoat sprays on the market, available in a variety of colours. Although most are useful, I recommend Games Workshop ones. Although a bit more expensive than the others, they are very reliable, you can control the paint flow easily to get a thinner or thicker coat and the paint is matt (I don't favour satin or glossy primers).

Brushes

There are a wide array of brushes for you to choose from. You'll find all types of materials and price ranges. In my opinion, the best (though the most expensive) are sable brushes. However, you can also get a hold of some high-quality synthetic brushes. Sable brushes tend to have soft bristles while the hair on synthetic brushes is stiffer. As always, the best type of brush to use is the one that best suits your painting habits. Regarding size, brushes for painting miniatures range from 2 (the thickest) to 5/0 (the finest). The sizes I use most are 1 (especially for base colours) and 0 (for highlighting and details), though occasionally I use a 3/0 (for fine details). Besides the traditional pointed brushes, flat brushes are especially useful for 'drybrushing' (see 'Highlighting Techniques' in Chapter Two).

Varnishes

There are two types of varnish to choose from: water- or solvent-based. Added to this, we have the choice of three kinds of finish: matt, satin or high-gloss. Solvent-based varnishes usually provide better protection and tend to have more of a matt finish. As we will see later, I highly recommend you varnish all of your painted figures.

Glues

There are quite a few different types of glue to choose from. You should have three of them on hand: cyanoacrylate ('superglue'), multi-purpose contact glue and white glue (PVA). Use cyanoacrylate, the quickest-drying of the three for gluing metal or plastic pieces together. This adhesive is very strong and toxic, so be careful. Once dry (which is practically instantly), the adhesive crystallizes between the two pieces, which means that any hard blow (such as dropping a figure on the floor) will break the bond. Contact glue is more useful for attaching figures to the temporary base we'll use when painting as well as to the figure's permanent base. After applying contact glue, it's a good idea to wait a few seconds before putting the pieces together, as this will optimize its sticking power. It takes a little while to dry, but the bond is a lot more solid than cyanoacrylate. The only way to separate the pieces is by cutting the glue with a modelling knife. White glue (diluted) is used to attach the sand or artificial grass that will decorate the figure's permanent base.

Supports

Before painting our miniatures, we need to attach them to some kind of support (Figure 2). This will allow us to hold and angle the figures as we wish while painting, without having to the touch the figure at all. There are two basic supports we can use: strips of wood or plastic containers (such as empty painting pots or old film canisters). I recommend using wooden strips around 30cm long, 2cm wide for 15mm miniatures or 3-4cm for

(Figure 2)

28mm miniatures, and no more than 1cm thick. This will make them more stable since the width is greater than the height. The strips are our best bet if we are going to 'mass-produce' figures with similar or identical uniforms. Now, if we're only going to paint one figure at a time, plastic containers are more appropriate. But, you should experiment and use whichever is most comfortable for you. For painting shields, we can use either method: if we use wooden strips, hammer headless nails into them to stick the shields onto; if we opt for empty paint pots, glue on a piece of plastic sprue and use this as a supporting arm. Use superglue to secure the shield to the support as this can be easily removed once we've finished.

Painter's Palette

As obvious as it may seem, having a good palette to put and mix our colours on is very important. You can choose what you like best, anything from plastic plates, porcelain appetiser dishes or professional palettes (there are very cheap plastic ones). The latter is the best option as its useful concave holes preserve paint for longer (they dry faster over a flat surface). Since acrylics become fairly waterproof when they dry, we won't have any problems mixing new paint on top of older dry paint.

Modelling Tools

At the minimum we should have modelling knives, a hand drill with different sized bits and some files. Also it will be useful to have tweezers, pliers and scissors easily to hand.

PAINTING SPACE

I know that not everyone has the opportunity to have a permanent painting space. In my early years I had to wander around carrying all my stuff from one place to the other (from one room to the kitchen, from the kitchen to another room, like a paint nomad). Needless to say, to have a permanent painting space appropriately furnished (close to references books, with a radio for company and some room for a laptop) doesn't just save us time and hassle but adds extra motivation to paint.

SOME BASIC CONCEPTS

How do I handle the brush?

We need precise brushstrokes – we're not trying to be Van Gogh! – so the closer to the point we handle the brush, the better. Just think of it as a pen that we are going to 'write' with on the figure.

How do I clean the brush?

Taking good care of your brushes is a must if you want to keep them in good condition for a long time. The best way to do this is to clean them properly. Normally, all you need to do when using acrylics is put the brush in water and shake it a bit. But, if you see there is paint still stuck on the bristles, you can rest the brush on the side of the jar and gently twist it. Don't ever clean the brush on the bottom of the jar and, of course, never store your brush inside the water-filled jar. Always use toilet paper or paper towels to dry your brushes with, never ever use rags or any type of cloth.

Shake it, baby!

All paints have a mixed composition of pigment and diluent. This is especially obvious when you take a bottle that has been stored for a long time and can see that the two have separated. So, anytime we are using any paint, especially if new or after a long storage, we have to vigorously shake the bottle to mix the paint properly. If the paint we put in the palette is oily or has traces of white, shake it again until it becomes fully homogeneous.

If the paint is not properly shaken it will dry with a glossy sheen.

Should I add water to the paint?

Yes, indeed. Unless we are painting some very specific details requiring a lot of precision (such as eyes), the paint needs water to flow better. Moreover, when we paint units of figures we could spend some time working with the same colour, so adding water will prevent it drying out.

How do I mix colours?

Here's my tip: don't drop the paint *onto* the mix. Doing so allows no control over the mix and could easily over-lighten the colour you're trying to create. Instead, drop the paint *beside* the mix, and blend the colours progressively. Once you have reached the right shade, remove the excess of paint.

Regarding the proportions of paint used when mixing, all the percentages offered in the colour charts of this book are highly approximate. It's impossible to offer exact figures and even so it would greatly depend on personal tastes. On the other hand, my own mixes change from one time to another; I don't view this as a problem as historical uniforms were not always precisely the same shade of colour (they wore out fast, were seldom or never washed, colours fade with rain and sun, and being on campaign adds yet more grime and dirt).

Drying times

Acrylic paints tend to dry quite fast but it depends on a series of circumstances, such as the amount of water added to the mix, temperature and humidity.

Matt or Satin?

I'm a firm advocate of a matt finish for figures, or at least as matt as possible: I'm not a matt paint fundamentalist! I always use matt colours but some of the step-by-step photos in this book have an artificially glossy effect produced by camera flash, especially on varnished figures.

HEALTHY PAINTING

Whether painting miniatures is a hobby or a job for you, you should take into consideration a number of factors to help both yourself and the environment.

Chemicals

I exclusively use acrylics as explained before: they are good paints, easier to use and faster to dry than enamels, and they are odourless and better for the environment (as they need no toxic thinners or solvents). However, I do use non-acrylic sprays and varnishes. Today sprays are CFC free, but some propellants, varnishes and thinners such as turpentine are still toxic.

My advice is to avoid the use of toxic products as much as possible. If you do use them, never pour the remnants down the toilet; if possible, always dispose of the residue in the locally approved manner (in the UK, take it to your local waste disposal site and check which area to put it in). And, always use the sprays in well-ventilated areas such as on a balcony, by an open window, a shed or garage with the door open or even in the garden.

Lights

Painting can be tiring for your eyes. Although I have suffered from myopia since my childhood, I didn't have problems until recently. Now that I'm in my mid-30s, my eyes begin to get tired easily and faster, so I've started to value what proper lighting can offer. First of all, although I have painted at night many times, I prefer to paint with indirect daylight. Although some painters prefer to paint using natural daylight, this didn't work for me. I'm lucky to live in sunny Spain, where we have many hours of daylight, even in winter, but whatever daylight is available you will also need a good electric light system. You should use two lamps, one to offer a general light to your whole working area, the other to supplement this with light directly where you're painting. I have tried many different bulbs over the years. Halogen lights are very powerful, but in my case they were painful for my eyes and very hot to work under (during the Spanish summer this is a huge issue to consider!). Besides the obvious environmental benefits, low-energy bulbs generate no heat but maybe won't offer enough light to paint by. To summarize, take advantage of daylight as much as possible and use two lamps: an area light and a direct light, using low-energy bulbs if possible.

Yoga

If you are planning to spend long hours painting, you need to do some exercise. As a full-time painter, working eight or more hours a day, I started to experience physical problems, especially in my back. Muscle spasms started to be commonplace, as well as lumbar pain. One day I decided to try yoga. Leaving spiritual considerations aside, I discovered that yoga is the perfect physical practice for painters. It's not an aerobic exercise so you don't need to be in good shape (a painter's life is quite sedentary!) but on the other hand it offers two essential benefits: building up and stretching. The building up is slow and progressive, but it will strengthen your back and prevent spasms. Also, stretching the muscles of arms, legs and back will be necessary (and even delightful) after a long painting journey. After eight years of yoga my only regret is not having started before! However, you don't need to be a yogi to experience the benefits of the practice; there are some easy asanas such as Adho Mukha that everybody can do at home and which have immediate benefits.

2

How To Paint Miniatures

This chapter explains every painting technique I use. Instead of a boring theoretical explanation, let's get practical and learn how to paint miniatures by painting one. And what a beautiful specimen this Relic Miniatures Pyrrhus is (Figure 3) … so we'll use it as an example. This outstanding multi-part miniature needs some assembling, although it's quite simple (just be careful not to cut the horse's reins off by mistake); there is an assembly guide on the Relic Miniatures website.

(Figure 3)

(Figure 4)

THE UNDERCOAT

Any painting work starts with a simple decision: white or black undercoat? However, which one we choose will define both the whole painting process and the final result. Both options have pros and cons:

White undercoat

Pros: Details on the figure can be seen easily and paint covers white better (Figure 4), even for problematic colours such as white, yellow or red; painting the base colours is easier and faster and final result is brighter.

Cons: Figures can look too flat so some kind of lining, wash or patina is often added (if not absolutely necessary) to separate the different colour areas.

Black undercoat

Pros: The undercoat serves as a lining that helps to separate colour areas and gives contrast to our figures. This is the best option for metals.

Cons: Details on the figure can be a bit difficult to see and some colours need a couple of layers to cover the undercoat properly; painting the base colours can be slower as we have to keep the a black line between separate colour areas, and final result looks darker than using a white undercoat.

As seen in the Pyrrhus figure (Figure 5), the two options are not mutually exclusive as white undercoat is better for some parts of the figure and black for others. In this particular case, my advice is to prime with a white spray and touch up with brushed black paint any areas missed by the spray (to provide shading on the finished figure).

(Figure 5)

BASE COLOURS

After the figure is primed, the next logical step is to paint the base colours. Some people prefer to paint all the base colours first and then add highlights as a separate step. This is not my recommendation. Unless working with patinas, I would rather paint a base colour and all of its highlights before moving to the next base colour.

As we have seen before, to paint the base colours over white priming is faster and much easier as we don't need to be careful to avoid going over the black lines that edge the figure's different painting areas. However, when painting over white we have to be sure to cover all the priming and leave no white showing through!

HIGHLIGHTING TECHNIQUES

Highlights

This is the most used technique throughout this book, whatever undercoat we use. The concept is quite easy: paint from inside to outside, from darker to lighter. But what are the key techniques? Where do we apply the brushstrokes? Which colours should we use and how many highlights do we need to do?

Let's take Pyrrhus' cloak as an example. First we paint the whole garment in Violet (960), darkened with a bit of Black (950). That will be our base colour (Figure 6). Once dry, we'll mix the base colour with Blue Violet (811) and paint over the base colour on the raised areas, leaving the base colour showing only in the pleats (Figure 7). We add more Blue Violet (811) to the previous mix and paint a second highlight over the first highlight, but paying attention just to the most prominent areas (Figure 8).

(Figure 6)

(Figure 7)

(Figure 8)

Although you could add extra highlights, two is enough in this case as it's not an especially large area. As we'll see, this rule of two highlights applies in most cases.

Sounds easy, right? Sadly, it's not always so simple! What about painting horses, for example, where the painting surface is larger and plainer? As a general rule larger painting areas would demand more highlights, and plainer surfaces would require fewer highlights (Figure 9). As before, paint from the inside to the outside and from darker to lighter, but learning where to paint the brushstrokes isn't as easy to get right. Painting experience and common sense are our best allies.

(Figure 9)

Lining

This technique is exactly the opposite of highlighting as the concept is to paint from the outside to the inside and from lighter to darker. It's very useful when painting larger sized figures such as 54mm, where you start with a base colour in the middle and then paint both highlights and linings, but in my opinion its use is very limited in wargame scales, mainly limited to correcting mistakes or separating colour areas.

In the case of Pyrrhus' horse, we didn't undercoat the reins in Black (950) as in all probability they will be touched by mistake when painting the horse. Although the reins will be painted red, we should add thin black lines first to reinforce the separation of this colour area from the horse's body (Figure 10).

(Figure 10)

Drybrushing is a very easy and effective technique, consisting of painting highlights over an undercoat but not with the usual brushstrokes. Dip the brush in the colour or mix of colours we will use for the highlights (Figure 11) but, instead of going straight to the figure, dab – or 'dry clean'– the brush on some tissue paper (Figure 12). This will absorb most of the paint ... but not all of it. This way, there will still be some paint on the brush, but it won't run or drip off. Now go to the figure and 'wipe' the whole area to paint with the brush (Figure 13). As the brush is mainly dry, the little paint that remains on it will highlight only the raised areas (Figure 14). Given its simplicity, the drybrush technique is perfect for a fast paint style, but not suitable for a quality finish except to work on very specific areas, either rough or textured (such as chainmail, terrain, furs or horses tails and manes) or especially plain (cannon or wagon woodwork).

There are some differences compared to regular highlighting: one highlight would be enough in most cases,

(Figure 11)

(Figure 12)

(Figure 13)

and never more than two. On the other hand, colours don't look as strong as they should look because of the 'wiping', so be sure that the contrast between base colours and highlights is strong. Finally, it must be noted that brushes suffer a lot when using this technique so, to avoid shortening the lives of our first-team players, I

(Figure 14)

recommend either buying specially designed brushes (with wide, plain and square points) or keeping old or worn out brushes for drybrushing (square the point with scissors for a better performance). Drybrushing is indicated in the colour charts as '*db*'.

In Pyrrhus' case, we'll use the drybrush technique to paint his horse's mane and tail, his helmet's horsehair and the terrain around the figure.

Washes

If lining is the opposite to highlighting, washes are the opposite to drybrushing! While drybrushing highlights the raised areas, a paint wash shades deep zones or recesses. It's an easy technique to shade a specific colour area with watered-down paint. Like drybrushing, however, in my painting system its use is limited to rough areas and maybe metals.

How does it work? First, paint the base colour, and then add a lot of water to the colour we are using for the wash. There are two ways to control the final level of darkness: by the colour itself and by the amount of water we add to it. Although a single wash is usually enough, several layers can be applied to get a progressive effect. Washes are indicated in the colour charts with a 'w'.

Returning to Phyrrus, we paint his leopard skin saddlecloth with Iraqi Sand (819), a very light colour (Figure 15). Once dry, we'll prepare a mix with Light

(Figure 15)

(Figure 16)

(Figure 17)

(Figure 18)

(Figure 19)

33

Brown (929) and Hull Red (985) and add a lot of water. As leopard skins are lighter around the edges, we'll give it three coats of brown wash, the first covering all the skin (Figure 16). Once dry we'll add a bit more Hull Red (985) to the mix (and some extra water) and wash over the first layer, but this time leaving the edges apart (Figure 17). Once dry, we'll repeat one more time with more Hull Red (985) and more water, but this time washing only the upper part of the skin (Figure 18). Once everything is dry, we'll paint the leopard spots with Black (950) mixed with Mahogany Brown (846), also very watered down (Figure 19). Phyrrus is now finished (Figures 20-21).

(Figure 20)

(Figure 21)

Pyrrhus	Base colour	1st highlight	2nd highlight	3rd highlight
Cloak	Violet (960) 90% + Black (950) 10%	Violet (960) 80% + Blue Violet (811) 20%	1st highlight 70% + Blue Violet (811) 30%	
Cuirass & helmet	Shining Gold (61-63) 70% + Black (950) 30%	Base colour 10% + Shining Gold (61-63) 90%	Burnished Gold (61-62)	
Silver wreath	Chainmail (61-56) 80% + Black (950) 20%	Mithril Silver (61-55)		
Pyrrhus' flesh	Beige Brown (875)	Light Brown 70% (929) + Flat Flesh (955) 30%	1st highlight 10% + Flat Flesh (955) 90%	
Linen armour, boots, pteryges (strips hanging from edge of armour) & helmet's horsehair	Light Grey (990) 50% + Sienna (113) 50%	Base colour 50% + White (951) 50%	1st highlight 50% + White (951) 50%	
Reins & sword scabbard	Cavalry Brown (982)	Cavalry Brown (982) 50% + Red (947) 50%	Red (947)	
Horse's coat	Light Grey (990)	Light Grey (990) 50% + White (951) 50%	1st highlight 50% + White (951) 50%	White (951)
Tail & mane	Light Grey (990)	Light Grey (990) 30% + White (951) 70% db	White (951) db	
Leopard skin	Iraqi Sand (819)	Light Brown (929) 90% + Hull Red (985) 10% w	1st highlight 90% + Hull Red (985) 10% w	2nd highlight 90% + Hull Red (985) 10% w
Base	Chocolate Brown (872)	Sienna (113) db	Buff (976) db	

Note on interpreting the colour charts in this book: All the percentages indicated for mixes are highly approximate and depends on personal taste.

db = drybrush

w = wash

3

Using Patinas

Trends are not only for fashion victims, they exist in the world of wargame figure painting too! Soon after I started to paint, someone taught me to paint with a homemade patina involving a mix of varnish, a product called Bitumen of Judea and turpentine (Figure 22). At first I just primed my figures in white, painted the base colours and added this patina as a sort of multipurpose wash. However, with time I started to improve my technique, applying highlights over the patina once it dried. Although I never abandoned this system completely, after some years I moved back to my roots and the traditional techniques explained in the previous chapter. To my surprise, patinas have come back into fashion thanks to The Army Painter products. Patinas can be very useful and effective as they bring together the best aspects of white and black undercoats.

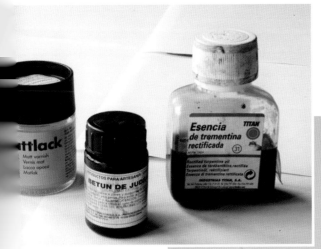

(Figure 22)

(Figure 24)

American War of Independence, Perry Miniatures and Eureka Miniatures, 28 mm. All these figures were painted with patinas.

BITUMEN OF JUDEA

'Bitumen of Judea' is the general term used to refer to a patina that actually involves other elements. First we put a coat of white primer on the figure and then we apply the base colours (Figure 23). This will be easier and quicker than over a black undercoat. Once we've finished this step, we prepare a mixture of solvent-based matt varnish (Marabú Mattlack is a good option), Bitumen of Judea and turpentine or white spirit (called 'mineral spirits' in the US) on a clean non-porous concave surface (plastic spoons are good). Bitumen of Judea, the key ingredient of

(Figure 25)

(Figure 26)

Late Roman Legio Palatina Herculani Seniores, Wargames Foundry, 28 mm.

this concoction, is very watery, glossy and extremely dark. Just a few drops added to the mix with a brush will do the job. The varnish will make up most of the mix; its two components, varnish and solvent/medium, must be mixed well before use. I recommend you stir it with the handle of an old brush instead of shaking it (Figure 24). The varnish performs several functions in this mixture: it gives the bitumen more body, helps it adhere to the surface, reduces its degree of darkness and gives a matt finish. If we want an extra-matt finish, we can take out some of the solvent/medium before mixing the components of the varnish (put it in a spare container, never throw it down the toilet). By removing a third or a quarter of the solvent, we'll increase the proportion of varnish in the container. I recommend doing this with newly purchased varnish as it has a tendency to settle and separate before being used. If you can't get your hands on Marabú varnish, you can use Titan's synthetic matt varnish (intended for use on wood) or many others.

Put some stirred varnish on the plastic spoon and add a few drops of Bitumen of Judea, with more or less quantity as required: more for darker colours, less for lighter ones (Figure 25). Lastly, we need to dilute the mixture so that it's not too thick. To do this, we can add a few drops of turpentine or white spirit with our brush (more if we removed part of the solvent/medium). After mixing everything together, we should get a very dark brown patina that's not very thick (Figure 26). We must now paint the figure with this patina; apply a generous coat on the entire figure but try to avoid excessive accumulations. This will give our figure an 'aged' effect and will also serve as a black undercoat or black lining since it accumulates more in the recesses (Figure 27). In other words, it's a wash (see 'Highlighting Techniques' in Chapter Two) that can be used for any colour. When it has dried, we'll be able to add highlights to the figure as we normally do (Figure 28). Remember that both the varnish and the Bitumen of Judea are soluble in solvent, so we'll have to clean the brush we use to apply the patina in turpentine or white spirit.

Late Roman Legio Palatina Iovani Seniores, Wargames Foundry (except the wounded guy in the middle, from Gripping Beast), 28 mm.

THE ARMY PAINTER

The Army Painter sells tins of ready-made patina of different shades, from light to dark. The concept is the same as described above, but there are a couple of differences from my homemade patina.

We save time as it is already mixed, but lose flexibility as we cannot regulate the degree of darkness according to our own taste. If we want variety, we could buy their complete range of patinas. While the finish of my own mix is matt (or at least should be if every step is properly followed), The Army Painter patinas are glossy, so we have to varnish in matt after. Despite these small differences, it works in the same way: paint the base colours over a white undercoat and apply the patina. Some people actually dip the figure in the tin, but I recommend the use of a brush. Once dried, varnish in matt (either brush or spray) before painting the highlights.

How to use the colour charts with patinas

All the colour charts included in this book are designed to paint with the usual base colour plus highlights over a white or black undercoat, but not involving patinas. The use of patinas will make our base colour darker once applied, so you should take this into consideration when painting the highlights. This is my advice:

Quality painting: *You can keep the same base colours indicated in the charts if you are using a light patina, but you should use a lighter base colour with darker patinas (unless you like dramatic contrasts!).*

Fast painting: *If you want to use a base colour plus patina without adding any highlights, use the colours or mixes indicated for the first or second highlights instead of the base colours.*

(Figure 23)

(Figure 27)

(Figure 28)

PART TWO
COLOURS

4

Black

Like many painters, I used to hate painting black. It was a real pain in the neck so I used to leave the black items (cartridges, shakoes, backpacks, belts, and so on) to the very end of a painting batch. I thought it was a plain and boring colour. I trust this chapter will show you how wrong this perception is!

Black is a colour full of possibilities. To demonstrate this I've chosen the figure of Jon Snow (Figure 29), one of the characters from the hugely popular *A Song of Ice and Fire*, written by George R. R. Martin. Jon Snow is a Brother

(Figure 29)

of the Night's Watch, an order of warriors who always dress completely in black. I will use this apparently black-only figure to demonstrate four different shades of black: clothes, furs, worn-out blackened leather and gleaming new blackened leather. Black will be the base colour in all cases, and highlights will make the difference. What I have aimed for is a figure with considerable diversity within a black palate yet sufficiently integrated to be appealing to the eye.

Although we always begin with black as the base colour, you can create diversity within your black palate by building highlights with greys, browns and blues. Further variation can be introduced through the use of metallic tones or mixing matt and gloss blacks. The resulting differences are sufficiently subtle to be true to an overall black effect, but make the final figure (and the painting process) more rewarding.

(Figures 30-31)

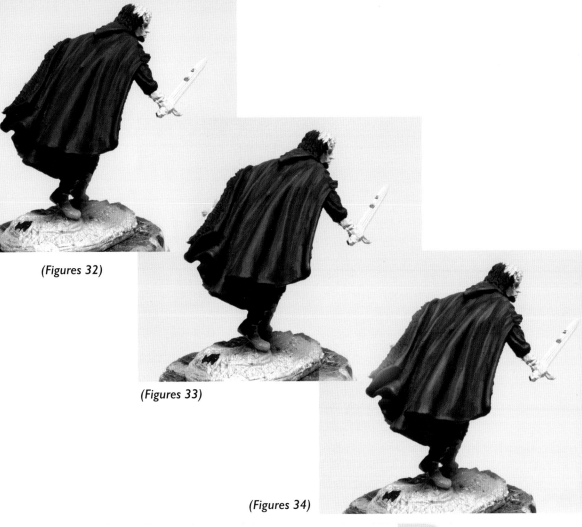

(Figures 32)

(Figures 33)

(Figures 34)

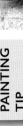

As a general rule, the darker and less contrasted the final result, the newer our cloth or leather will look, and the lighter or more contrasted the result, the more worn they will appear.

PAINTING TIP

STEP BY STEP

1. Clothes: To paint Jon's cloak, tunic and breeches we'll use a common and obvious colour combination: black highlighted by grey. However, as this is intended as a display rather than wargaming figure and the cloak is a big surface to paint, we'll apply three highlights instead of the usual two. Black (950) will be the obvious base colour (Figures 30-31), to which we'll progressively add Neutral Grey (992) for the first highlight (Figure 32), second highlight (Figure 33) and third highlight (Figure 34).

(Figures 35)

2. Furs and chainmail: The far north is a cold land to live and the defenders of The Wall must be warm, so furs are used aplenty. Obviously black fur could also be painted highlighted with grey, but we'll choose brown instead. The base colour will be Black (950) and we'll apply two highlights combining the base colour with Chocolate Brown (872) using the drybrush technique, but being careful not to mark the already painted clothes.

For the chainmail, although not really black, I wanted to give it a dark look. Here I combined several techniques: over the Gunmetal Grey (863) base colour I applied a wash of Black (950) and, once dry, a slight drybrush of Gunmetal Grey (863) (Figure 35).

3. Worn-out blackened leather: The books usually mention the Brothers of the Night's Watch clad in boiled leather armour. Although our figure wears mainly clothes and chainmail, the boots, gloves and belts could be painted as leather. The base colour will be Black (950), mixed with Mahogany Brown (846) for highlights. One highlight would

(Figures 36)   (Figures 37)

be enough for belts, but two will be needed for gloves and boots (Figure 36).

4. Gleaming leather: Only the sword scabbard remains, but it's enough to show you my final way to paint black. We have two options: to employ the same colour combination we used for clothes, but substituting flat for gloss black, or my favourite, which is to highlight the flat black with dark blue. One unique highlight will suffice in this case (Figure 37).

Jon Snow	Base colour	1st highlight	2nd highlight	3rd highlight
Clothes	Black (950)	Black (950) 80% + Neutral Grey (992) 20%	1st highlight 80 % + Neutral Grey (992) 20%	2nd highlight 80% + Neutral Grey (992) 20%
Cloak's lining	Black (950)	Black (950) 50% + Chocolate Brown (872) 50% db	Chocolate Brown (872) db	
Chainmail	Gunmetal Grey (863)	Black (950) w	Gunmetal Grey (863) db	
Leather	Black (950)	Black (950) 70% + Mahogany Brown 30% (846)	1st highlight 70% + Mahogany Brown (846) 30%	
Scabbard	Black (950)	Dark Prussian Blue (899)		

(Figures 38)

(Figures 39)

GHOST

I cannot finish this chapter without paying attention to Jon's inseparable companion: his direwolf, Ghost. The best way to paint the wolf's fur will be using the drybrush technique. As I mentioned in Chapter Two, colours don't look as strong as they should look due to the 'wiping' technique, so the contrast between base colours and highlights should be bold.

1. Instead of Light Grey (990), which is the standard base colour for painting white, we'll use Neutral Grey (992) as the base colour (Figure 38).

2. This will be followed by two consecutive drybrushings for the first highlight (Figure 39), with Neutral Grey (992) mixed with White (951) in equal amounts, and the second highlight (Figure 40) using just White (951).

3. Finally, we'll drybrush everything else (including paws, teeth, eyes), and the blood of Ghost's last victim (Figure 41).

(Figures 40)

(Figures 41)

Ghost	Base colour	1st highlight	2nd highlight
Fur	Neutral Grey (992)	Neutral Grey (992) 50% + White (951) 50% *db*	White (951) *db*
Paws & teeth	Sienna (113)	Tan Yellow (912)	Tan Yellow (912) 50% + White (951) 50%
Blood	Cavalry Brown (982) *db*	Red (947) *db*	

White

White is one of those colours considered difficult to use as it doesn't cover as well as some others, especially over a black undercoat. However, this really depends on the base colour and painting process used. In this chapter we'll learn not only how to paint white easily but also how to make different shades, from a pure clean white to a really worn out one: in real life, white shows up campaign grim and wear-and-tear far more easily than many other colours.

For this chapter we'll use several Capitan Games' Napoleonic Spanish infantry (Figure 42), wearing the 1805 regulation uniform used in 1808 (white with coloured regimental facings). However, at the start of the war many regiments hadn't received this uniform and still wore the 1802 regulation blue uniform with black facings (and two regiments hadn't even received the 1802 one by the start of the war!). On campaign, uniforms were rarely replaced and units had to improvise kit with whatever came to hand: this allows us to show different variations and alternative colour combinations in the figures we paint.

(Figure 42)

STEP BY STEP

For the step by step we'll use my standard method and colour combination to paint white. As usual we'll glue the figures onto empty paint bottles and, as white will be the predominant colour, we'll use a white undercoat.

1. We'll paint the base colour of all the areas that will be white, using Light Grey (990). Don't worry if paint gets

(Figure 43)

(Figure 44)

(Figure 45)

(Figure 46)

(Figure 47)

(Figure 4

(Figure 49)

onto non-white areas, as these will be repainted later (Figure 43). Before starting to paint any highlights, we'll do a black lining to separate the different colour areas (the coat from the waistcoat, the waistcoat from the breeches, and so on) and then we'll repaint with Black (950) all the non-white areas (Figures 44-45).

2. Now it's time for the highlights, adding White (951) to the base colour in equal parts for the first highlight (Figures 46-47). On the second highlight, you could use pure White (951), but I prefer to use a mostly white mixture, adding a bit of the previous highlight mix (Figures

48-49). In my opinion, this look more realistic as otherwise the uniform would look too clean.

3. We won't pay attention to the rest of the figure's painting process here, so we go straight onto the belts. I use two different techniques to paint white belts depending on the effect I want to give them. The painting process is the same: base colour plus one highlight – this time pure White (951) – but what changes is the base colour. It could be Sky Grey (989) or Buff (976). I used the latter here, obtaining an interesting yellowish effect in the belts (Figures 50-51).

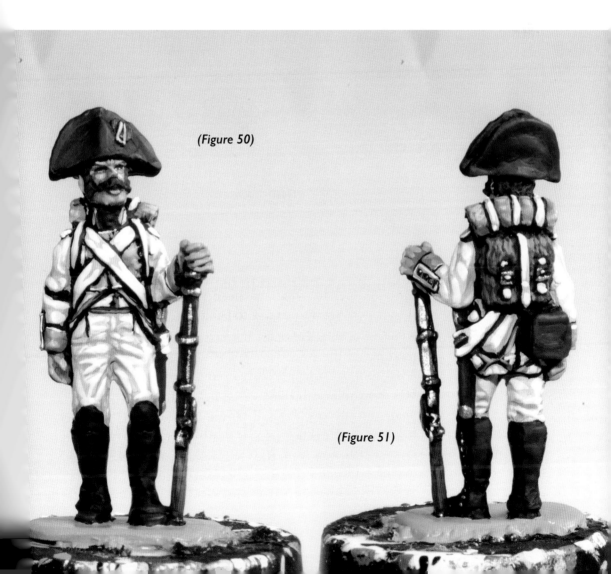

(Figure 50)

(Figure 51)

Spanish infantryman	Base colour	1st highlight	2nd highlight
Coat & breeches	Light Grey (990)	Light Grey (990) 50% + White (951) 50%	1st highlight 10% + White (951) 90%
Facings	Grey Blue (943) 60% + Prussian Blue (965) 40%	Base colour 70% + White (951) 30%	1st highlight 70% + White (951) 30%
Bicorn, gaiters, cartridge box & bayonet scabbard	Black (950)	Black (950) 80% + Neutral Grey (992) 20%	1st highlight 80% + Neutral Grey (992) 20%
Shoes	Black (950)	Black (950) 70% + Mahogany Brown (846) 30%	
Knapsack	Chocolate Brown (872)	Beige Brown (875)	
Blanket	Neutral Grey (992) 70% + Beige Brown (875) 30%	Base colour + White (951) 30%	1st highlight + White (951) 30%
Musket	Hull Red (985)	Mahogany Brown (846)	
Belts	Buff (976)	White (951)	
Iron	Chainmail (61-56)		
Brass	Shining Gold (61-63)		

MILICIAS PROVINCIALES OFFICER

In the step by step, I suggested not painting the second highlight with pure white but instead adding a bit of the mixture of the previous highlight. Well, for this officer's coat we'll use a lighter base colour, Sky Grey, add White 951 for the first highlight and this time we actually will paint the second highlight with pure white, to achieve a brighter finish (Figure 52). For the breeches, mix Light Grey (990) and Raw Sienna (113) for the base colour, adding white progressively for the highlights. Tan Yellow (912) could be used instead, but you may find it too bright.

(Figure 52)

Officer	Base colour	1st highlight	2nd highlight
Coat	Sky Grey (989)	Sky Grey (989) 50% + White (951) 50%	White (951)
Breeches	Light Grey (990) 50% + Raw Sienna (113) 50%	Base colour 50% + White (951) 50%	1st highlight 50% + White (951) 50%
Facings	Cavalry Brown (982)	Cavalry Brown (982) 50% + Red (947) 50%	Red (947) 90% + Scarlet (817) 10%
Bicorn, boots & sword scabbard	Black (950)	Black (950) 80% + Neutral Grey (992) 20%	1st highlight 80% + Neutral Grey (992) 20%

SERGEANT

The coat and breeches of this sergeant will be painted in the same way as the officer, using Sky Grey (989) as the base colour (Figure 53). Sky Grey (989) was also used as the base colour for the belts.

Sergeant	Base colour	1st highlight	2nd highlight
Coat & breeches	Sky Grey (989)	Sky Grey (989) 50% + White (951) 50%	White (951)
Belts	Sky Grey (989)	White (951)	
Facings	Prussian Blue (965) 90% + Black (950) 10%	Prussian Blue (965) 90% + White (951) 10%	1st highlight 80% + White (951) 20%
Bicorn, gaiters & sword scabbard	Black (950)	Black (950) 80% + Neutral Grey (992) 20%	1st highlight 80% + Neutral Grey (992) 20%

(Figure 53)

DRUMMER

With the drummer's coat I wanted to represent a worn-out look, so I mixed Light Grey (990) and Raw Sienna (113) for the base colour, adding white progressively for the highlights (Figure 54). I used a different base colour, Buff (976) and Sky Grey (989), for the drum and sword belts respectively.

Drummer	Base colour	1st highlight	2nd highlight
Coat	Light Grey (990) 50% + Sienna (113) 50%	Base colour 50% + White (951) 50%	1st highlight 50% + White (951) 50%
Facings	Grey Blue (943) 60% + Prussian Blue (965) 40%	Base colour 70% + White (951) 30%	1st highlight 70% + White (951) 30%
Drum belt	Sky Grey (989)	White (951)	
Sword belt	Buff (976)	White (951)	

(Figure 54)

INFANTRYMAN

Finally, this infantryman wears a combination of garments of different whites, a coat painted like the step by step and a worn-out breeches painted like the drummer's coat (Figure 55). Again, belts were painted using Buff (976) as the base colour.

Infantryman	Base colour	1st highlight	2nd highlight
Coat	Light Grey (990)	Light Grey (990) 50% + White (951) 50%	1st highlight 10% + White (951) 90%
Breeches	Light Grey (990) 50% + Raw Sienna (113) 50%	Base colour 50% + White (951) 50%	1st highlight 50% + White (951) 50%
Facings	Black (950)	Black (950) 80% + Neutral Grey (992) 20%	1st highlight 80% + Neutral Grey (992) 20%
Belts	Buff (976)	White (951)	

(Figure 55)

6

Blue

Perry Miniatures' Napoleon and Staff at Waterloo set is perfect to show how to paint three different shades of blue: the darkest indigo wore by generals, the sky blue of the Imperial Orderlies and the grey-blue of the 3rd Hussars (Figure 56). Of course, these colour combinations aren't exclusively Napoleonic and are applicable to other periods.

We'll also pay attention to gold and silver thread: the cloth sashes, epaulettes and other embroideries that decorated many uniforms in this period. Some people prefer to paint these insignias of rank with metallic paints, but I favour the use of non-metallic colours with the addition of some metallic brushstrokes at the very end of the process. The higher the rank, the more gold those insignias contain, so a few brushstrokes would be enough for a junior officer or even a colonel, but a general would need considerably more.

(Figure 56)

DROUOT

Dark blue is probably the most commonly used uniform colour since their development in the middle of the seventeenth century. Albeit with minor shade variations, Prussians, post-Revolution French and US Federals all wore dark blue. As an example, we'll paint General Drouot, Napoleon's artillery commander.

1. Over the black undercoat, we'll paint the base colour (Figure 57) with a mix of Prussian Blue (965) and Black (950), to be followed by a first highlight (Figure 58) with Prussian Blue (965) and a second highlight (Figures 59-60) with Prussian Blue (965) plus White (951).

2. Once the blue is finished we'll paint the gold thread, using Beige Brown (875) as the base colour. French generals had a code of colours to distinguish their status: white for marshals, red for divisional generals and sky blue for brigadier generals. As a divisional general, we'll paint red diagonals on Drouot's sash (Figure 61). For the first highlight we could mix Beige Brown (875) with Yellow Ochre (813) in equal parts, or skip this mix and use Raw Sienna (113) instead. Note that by painting this highlight

(Figure 57)   (Figure 58)   (Figure 59)   (Figure 60)

(Figure 61) (Figure 62) (Figure 63) (Figure 64)

we transform the red lines into squares (Figure 62). Now it's time for the second highlight (Figure 63), using Yellow Ochre (813). Note that the epaulettes' fringes, where the first highlight was painted with vertical brushstrokes, is now painted with horizontal ones to represent each individual braid. The sash is now highlighted with Red (947). Finally, small and precise spare brushstrokes of Burnished Gold (61-62) are painted here and there over all the golden areas (Figures 64-65).

3. We'll paint the other colours to complete the figure (Figures 66-67).

As a high-ranking officer, I employed a very dark blue to represent the good quality of his uniform. In the case of French rank and file, whose uniforms were rarely brand new and often lost their colour due to weathering, we could choose a lighter shade, starting with a Prussian Blue (965) with less added black as base colour, and adding white instead of blue in the first highlight to get a pastel or off-blue tone.

(Figure 65)   *(Figure 66)*   *(Figure 67)*

Drouot	Base colour	1st highlight	2nd highlight	3rd highlight
Coat & breeches	Prussian Blue (965) 80% + Black (950) 20%	Prussian Blue (965)	Prussian Blue (965) 80% + White (951) 20%	
Gold thread	Beige Brown (875)	Raw Sienna (113)	Yellow Ochre (913)	Burnished Gold (61-62)
Reds	Cavalry Brown (982)	Red (947)		
Boots & bicorn	Black (950)	Black (950) 80% + Neutral Grey (992) 20%	1st highlight 80% + Neutral Grey (992) 20%	
Boots (lower part)	Black (950)	Black (950) 70% + Mahogany Brown (846)	1st highlight 70% + Raw Sienna (113) 30%	
Gloves	Light Grey (990) 50% + Sienna (113) 50%	Base colour 50% + White (951) 50%	1st highlight 50% + White (951) 50%	
Silver	Chainmail (61-56)	Mithril Silver (61-55)		
Gold	Shining Gold (61-63)	Burnished Gold (61-62)		

GOURGAUD

Although not as common in Napoleonic uniforms as dark blue, sky blue was used, for example, by the Bavarian Army, for Hungarian breeches and in some specific uniforms such as the French Imperial Officiers D'Ordonnance. Sky blue looks smart on Oriental costumes and Western civilian clothes, especially for women.

1. Over the black undercoat, we'll paint the base colour (Figure 68) with a mix of Grey Blue (943) and Prussian Blue (965) in equal proportions. We'll progressively add

(Figure 68)   *(Figure 69)*   *(Figure 70)*   *(Figure 71)*

(Figure 72)   *(Figure 73)*   *(Figure 74)*   *(Figure 75)*

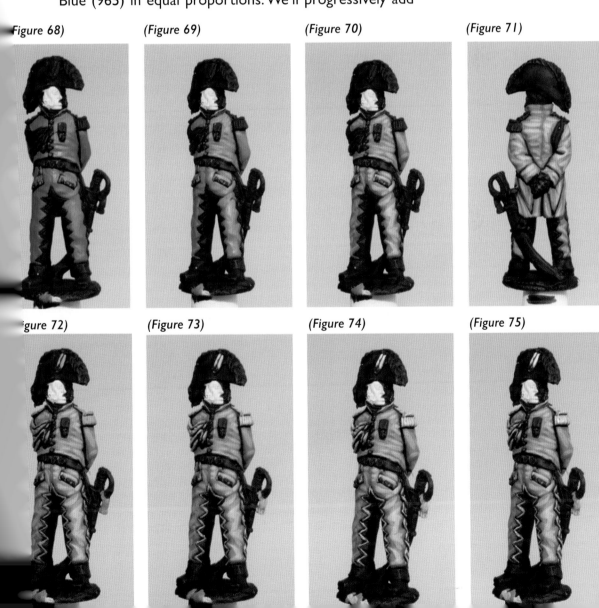

(Figure 76)   *(Figure 77)*   *(Figure 78)*   *(Figure 79)*

White (951) for the first highlight (Figure 69) and the second highlight (Figures 70-71).

2. For the silver thread, we'll use Neutral Grey (992) as the base colour (Figure 72). The highlights will be painted as with Drouot, but using Light Grey (990) for the first highlight (Figure 73), Sky Grey (989) for the second highlight (Figure 74) and Mithril Silver (61-55) for the final metallic touches (Figures 75-76).

3. We'll paint the other colours to complete the figure (Figures 77-79).

Gourgaud	Base colour	1st highlight	2nd highlight	3rd highlight
Coat & trousers	Grey Blue (943) 50% + Prussian Blue (965) 50%	Base colour 80% + White (951) 20%	1st highlight 70% + White (951) 30%	
Silver thread	Neutral Grey (992)	Light Grey (990)	Sky Grey (989)	Mithril Silver (61-55)
Reds	Cavalry Brown (982)	Red (947)		
Bicorn & boots	Black (950)	Black (950) 80% + Neutral Grey (992) 20%	1st highlight 80% + Neutral Grey (992) 20%	
Trouser reinforcements	Black (950)	Black (950) 70% + Mahogany Brown (846)	1st highlight 70% + Raw Sienna (113) 30%	
Silver	Chainmail (61-56)	Mithril Silver (61-55)		

As Napoleon's Orderly, Gourgaud's uniform has to look brighter and more impressive than, for example, a Bavarian private. To make a worn-out sky blue uniform, add less Prussian Blue (965) to the Grey Blue (943) in the base colour, or just use the colour combination demonstrated on the hussar below.

ADC, 3RD HUSSARS

The last combination we'll show is a grey-blue uniform, present in some Napoleonic regiments (such as the 3rd Hussars) and artillery train drivers, but also on American Civil War Union and Confederate trousers. It's also a useful colour for ancient and medieval armies, where I favour off-colours rather than strong ones.

1. Over the black undercoat, we'll paint the base colour (Figure 80) with a mix of French Mir Blue (900) – or Grey Blue (943) – and Black (950). We'll progressively add White (951) for the first highlight (Figure 81) and the second highlight (Figures 82-83).

2. For the silver thread, we'll use Neutral Grey (992) as the base colour. The highlights will be painted as with Gourmand, using Light Grey (990) for the first highlight, Sky Grey (989) for the second highlight and Mithril Silver (61-55) for the final metallic touches.

(Figure 80)   (Figure 81)   (Figure 82)   (Figure 83)

(Figure 84)   *(Figure 85)*

3. We'll paint the other colours to complete the figure (Figures 84-85). Note that the red colour of the armband indicates that he's an ADC attached to a divisional general.

ADC 3rd Hussars	Base colour	1st highlight	2nd highlight	3rd highlight
Coat & trousers	French Mir Blue (900) or Grey Blue (943) 90% + Black (950) 10%	Base colour 80% + White (951) 20%	1st highlight 80% + White (951) 20%	
Silver thread	Neutral Grey (992)	Light Grey (990)	Sky Grey (989)	Mithril Silver (61-55)
Shako & cuffs	Cavalry Brown (982)	Cavalry Brown (982) 50% + Red (947) 50%	Red (947)	
Shako reinforcements, sabretache & cartridge box	Black (950)	Black (950) 80% + Neutral Grey (992) 20%	1st highlight 80% + Neutral Grey (992) 20%	
Boots	Black (950)	Black (950) 70% + Mahogany Brown (846)	1st highlight 70% + Raw Sienna (113) 30%	
Silver	Chainmail (61-56)	Mithril Silver (61-55)		
Gold	Shining Gold (61-63)	Burnished Gold (61-62)		

NAPOLEON

(Figure 86)   *(Figure 87)*

Napoleon	Base colour	1st highlight	2nd highlight	3rd highlight
Overcoat	Neutral Grey (992) 80% + Black (950) 20%	Base colour 80% + White (951) 20%	1st highlight 80% + White (951) 20%	2nd highlight 80% + White (951) 20%
Coat	Military Green (975) 90% + Black (950) 10%	Base colour 80% + Iraqui Sand (819) 20%	1st highlight 80% + Iraqui Sand (819) 20%	
Breeches & waistcoat	Sky Grey (989)	Sky Grey (989) 50% + White (951) 50 %	White (951)	
Gloves	Light Grey (990) 50% + Sienna (113) 50%	Base colour 50% + White (951) 50%	1st highlight 50% + White (951) 50%	
Reds	Cavalry Brown (982)	Cavalry Brown (982) 50% + Red (947) 50%	Red (947)	
Bicorn & boots	Black (950)	Black (950) 80% + Neutral Grey (992) 20%	1st highlight 80% + Neutral Grey (992) 20%	
Gold	Shining Gold (61-63)	Burnished Gold (61-62)		

NEY

(Figure 88)

(Figure 89)

(Figure 90)

Ney	Base colour	1st highlight	2nd highlight	3rd highlight
Coat	Prussian Blue (965) 80% + Black (950) 20%	Prussian Blue (965)	Prussian Blue (965) 80% + White (951) 20%	
Gold thread	Beige Brown (875)	Raw Sienna (113)	Yellow Ochre (913)	Burnished Gold (61-62)
Breeches	Light Grey (990)	Light Grey (990) 50% + White (951) 50 %	1st highlight 10% + White (951) 90%	
Gloves	Light Grey (990) 50% + Sienna (113) 50%	Base colour 50% + White (951) 50%	1st highlight 50% + White (951) 50%	
Band	Cavalry Brown (982)	Cavalry Brown (982) 50% + Red (947) 50%	Red (947)	
Boots & sword scabbard	Black (950)	Black (950) 80% + Neutral Grey (992) 20%	1st highlight 80% + Neutral Grey (992) 20%	
Silver	Chainmail (61-56)	Mithril Silver (61-55)		
Gold	Shining Gold (61-63)	Burnished Gold (61-62)		

SOULT

(Figure 91)

(Figure 92)

Soult (Figures 91-92)	Base colour	1st highlight	2nd highlight	3rd highlight
Coat	Prussian Blue (965) 80% + Black (950) 20%	Prussian Blue (965)	Prussian Blue (965) 80% + White (951) 20%	
Gold thread	Beige Brown (875)	Raw Sienna (113)	Yellow Ochre (913)	Burnished Gold (61-62)
Breeches	Light Grey (990)	Light Grey (990) 50% + White (951) 50 %	1st highlight 10% + White (951) 90%	
Gloves	Light Grey (990) 50% + Sienna (113) 50%	Base colour 50% + White (951) 50%	1st highlight 50% + White (951) 50%	
Band	Cavalry Brown (982)	Cavalry Brown (982) 50% + Red (947) 50%	Red (947)	
Boots & bicorn	Black (950)	Black (950) 80% + Neutral Grey (992) 20%	1st highlight 80% + Neutral Grey (992) 20%	
Bicorn feathers	Light Grey (990)	White (951)		
Boots (lower part)	Black (950)	Black (950) 70% + Mahogany Brown (846)	1st highlight 70% + Raw Sienna (113) 30%	
Silver	Chainmail (61-56)	Mithril Silver (61-55)		
Gold	Shining Gold (61-63)	Burnished Gold (61-62)		

7

Red

There are less shades of red than certain other colours such as blue or brown. Most of the time I use pretty much the same colour combination when painting red, with just a few differences.

To demonstrate painting red I'm using Front Rank's late-seventeenth-century English soldiers. This will allow me to paint different shades of red depending on the quality of the uniform, from an officer to a private, including two sergeants. With the exception of the officer, all of the figures will have a very similar painting process.

Red is one of the most difficult colours to photograph, especially when using a flash. The photos shown here look glossier than they are when viewed with the naked eye and the highlighting sequence looks much less contrasted than it actually is. Thus, some of the colour combinations and variations won't be properly appreciated in the photographs, but following my painting steps will look great on your own figures.

POINTING SERGEANT

The red coats of English soldiers were not actually red but more of a scarlet or brick red. However, sergeants could wear better quality uniforms than the rank and file, and this allows me to use this figure as an example of the standard colour combination I use to produce a vivid red

(Figure 93)

(Figures 93-94). It's easy and requires minimum mixing. This colour combination would also be perfect for British Napoleonic officers and generals.

1. Paint the base colour (Figure 95) using Cavalry Brown (982).

2. For the first highlight (Figure 96), mix Cavalry Brown (982) and Red (947) in equal parts.

3. Paint the second highlight (Figures 97-98) with Red (947).

(Figure 94)

(Figure 95)

(Figure 96)

(Figure 97)

(Figure 98)

Sergeant	Base colour	1st highlight	2nd highlight
Coat	Cavalry Brown (982)	Cavalry Brown (982) 50% + Red (947) 50%	Red (947)
Facings, breeches & stockings	Prussian Blue (965) 80% + Black (950) 20%	Prussian Blue (965)	Prussian Blue (965) 80% + White (951) 20%
Hat	Black (950)	Black (950) 80% + Neutral Grey (992) 20%	1st highlight 80% + Neutral Grey (992) 20%
Shoes & sword scabbard	Black (950)	Black (950) 70% + Mahogany Brown (846)	1st highlight 70% + Raw Sienna (113) 30%

MARCHING PRIVATE

Once we've mastered the standard red shown above, let's start to apply a series of variations starting with the usual colour combination I use for English or British redcoats of any period. We'll use the marching private as an example (Figures 99-100).

1. The base colour (Figure 101) and first highlight (Figure 102) are exactly the same as in the previous example, but the second highlight will make the difference.

2. As before, the second highlight would be Red (947), but we'll add some Scarlet (817) to give it an orange effect (Figures 103-104). If this is too vivid for your taste or you would like to obtain a more realistic final effect, add a little of the remaining paint from the first highlight if still fresh, or a pinch of Cavalry Brown (982) if not.

(Figure 99)

(Figure 100)

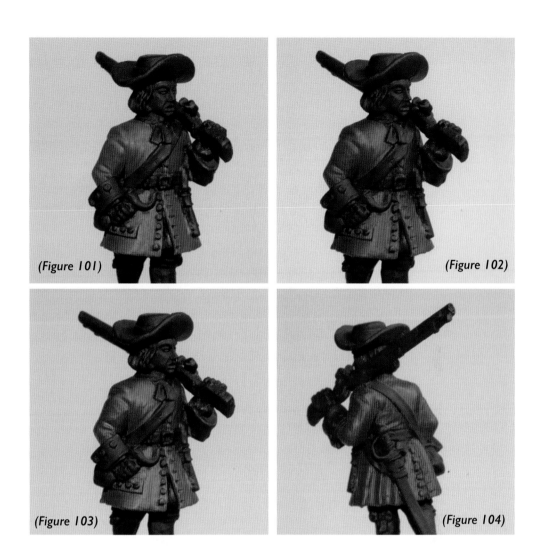

(Figure 101)

(Figure 102)

(Figure 103)

(Figure 104)

Private	Base colour	1st highlight	2nd highlight
Coat	Cavalry Brown (982)	Cavalry Brown (982) 50% + Red (947) 50%	1st highlight 10% + Red (947) 80% + Scarlet (817) 10%
Facings & stockings	Prussian Blue (965) 80% + Black (950) 20%	Prussian Blue (965)	Prussian Blue (965) 80% + White (951) 20%
Breeches & belts	Chocolate Brown (872)	Chocolate Brown (872) 50% + Beige Brown (875) 50%	Beige Brown (875)
Hat & bayonet scabbard	Black (950)	Black (950) 80% + Neutral Grey (992) 20%	1st highlight 80% + Neutral Grey (992) 20%
Shoes & sword scabbard	Black (950)	Black (950) 70% + Mahogany Brown (846)	1st highlight 70% + Raw Sienna (113) 30%

STANDING SERGEANT

After experimenting with highlights, it's now time to experiment with the base colour on this model of a sergeant (Figures 105-106). Although Cavalry Brown (982) is a very good choice, you can also use a faded red.

1. Cavalry Brown (982) is too red and vivid for this faded effect, so for an alternative shade I recommend adding a bit of Chocolate Brown (872) or similar (Figure 107).

2. For the first highlight (Figure 108) add Red (947) to the base colour, about 50%/50% as before.

3. The second highlight (Figures 109-110) would be similar to the private's one: Red (947) will still be the main colour but we'll substitute Scarlet (817) for a dash of any sandy colour, and optionally also a bit of the first highlight colour.

(Figure 105)

(Figure 106)

(Figure 107)

(Figure 108)

(Figure 109)

(Figure 110)

Sergeant	Base colour	1st highlight	2nd highlight
Coat	Cavalry Brown (982)+ Chocolate Brown (872)	Base colour 50% + Red (947) 50%	1st highlight 10% + Red (947) 80% + Iraqi Sand (819) 10%
Facings & breeches	Prussian Blue (965) 80% + Black (950) 20%	Prussian Blue (965)	Prussian Blue (965) 80% + White (951) 20%
Stockings	Light Grey (990) 50% + Sienna (113) 50%	Base colour 50% + White (951) 50%	1st highlight 50% + White (951) 50%
Hat & bayonet scabbard	Black (950)	Black (950) 80% + Neutral Grey (992) 20%	1st highlight 80% + Neutral Grey (992) 20%
Shoes & sword scabbard	Black (950)	Black (950) 70% + Mahogany Brown (846)	1st highlight 70% + Raw Sienna (113) 30%

OFFICER

In the late seventeenth century, officers wore very richly coloured uniforms with gold or silver embroidery. Instead of the common red coats of the rank and file, officers wore crimson clothes, sashes, bands and even had gloves and sword scabbards in that colour (Figures 111-112). Over time English (and later on, British) officers adopted red coats like their men (but better quality ones!), but they kept the crimson sashes as a reminiscence of these early uniforms. Crimson is not an easy-to-paint colour and requires some mixing. On the other hand, mixing gives us many options to get different shades.

1. As a start, instead of using just Cavalry Brown (982) as base colour, which we do as a general rule when painting red, we'll mix it with a bit of Hull Red (985). That way we'll get a dark reddish brown as a starting point (Figure 113).

2. For the first highlight we'll add either Red (947) to get a conventional dark red shade, Sunset Red (802) to get a rosier shade, or even better, both (Figure 114).

3. For the second highlight we'll repeat the procedure, this time adding Sunset Red (which gives a more vivid final result), White (which is paler but probably more realistic) or both. As usual, adapt these combinations to your own personal preference (Figure 115).

(Figure 111)

(Figure 112)

(Figure 113)

(Figure 114)

(Figure 115)

Officer	Base colour	1st highlight	2nd highlight	3rd highlight
Coat	Cavalry Brown (982) 80% + Hull Red (985) 20%	Base colour 50% + Sunset Red (802)/Red (947) 50%	1st highlight + Sunset Red (802)/White (951)	
Gold thread	Beige Brown (875)	Raw Sienna (113)	Yellow Ochre (913)	Burnished Gold (61-62)
Breeches & stockings	Neutral Grey (992) + Black (950)	Base Colour + White (951)	1st Highlight + White (951)	
Hat, shoes & sword scabbard	Black (950)	Black (950) 80% + Neutral Grey (992) 20%	1st highlight 80% + Neutral Grey (992) 20%	

(Figure 116)

8

Brown

Brown is one of those colours you can't avoid. Clothes, wood, leather, furs … there's always something brown to paint. Actually, I should say 'browns' rather than 'brown' as this specific colour has many different shades, from chocolate to buff, from reddish to greyish.

In order to show as many colour combinations as possible, I've chosen a Warlord Games' Thirty Years War gun with its crew (Figure 116). In that war the use of uniforms was limited to selected units (such as the Swedish Black, Yellow and Blue regiments). As a consequence, brown clothes were common amongst the armies' ranks of civilians and soldiers. As we are painting figures for wargaming we will employ the standard approach of two highlights over a base colour.

In general terms there are two groups – or families – of shades of brown:

Beige: *such as Chocolate Brown, Beige Brown and Tan Yellow.*

Red: *such as Hull Red, Cavalry Brown, Mahogany Brown and Saddle Brown.*

Colours within the same brown family mix well together (like Chocolate Brown with Beige Brown for furs or clothes, or Hull Red and Mahogany Brown for muskets) to get a very natural sequence of highlights, but combinations between colours of both families of browns and even other colours such as black or grey are also possible in order to achieve different shades. Finally, it's not only the base colour but also the highlight colour that determines the final result: the same base colour mixed with Tan Yellow or White will throw a quite different look!

PAINTING TIP

OFFICER

For the officer (Figures 117-118), who wears a better cut of cloth than his men, I choose Chocolate Brown (872) as a base colour (Figure 119), mixed progressively with Beige Brown (875) for the first highlight (Figure 120) and second highlight (Figures 121-122). These two colours of the same family marry very well and produce a smart and elegant brown. This is the colour combination I use most often for brown clothes.

The gloves were painted buff using the beige family as well. However, the leather belts were painted using the reddish family of colours. In both cases two highlights were painted, although one highlight would do well enough for belts.

(Figure 117)

(Figure 118)

(Figure 119)

(Figure 120)

(Figure 121)

(Figure 122)

Officer	Base colour	1st highlight	2nd highlight
Coat & breeches	Chocolate Brown (872)	Chocolate Brown (872) 50% + Beige Brown (875) 50%	1st highlight 10 % + Beige Brown (875) 90% or plain Beige Brown (875)
Gloves	Beige Brown (875)	Beige Brown (875) 50% + Iraqi Sand (819) 50%	1st highlight 50% + Iraqi Sand (819) 50%
Belts	Hull Red (985)	Saddle Brown (940)	Saddle Brown (940) 70% + Tan Yellow (912) 30%

(Figure 123)   (Figure 124)

MASTER GUNNER

As a specialist, the richness of his clothes is a sign of his status (Figures 123-124). For the master gunner I decided to combine two colours from different families: Beige Brown (875) with a pinch of Cavalry Brown (982) to get a vivid tone for the base colour (Figure 125), progressively mixed with Tan Yellow (912) for the first highlight (Figure 126) and second highlight (Figures 127-128).

Master gunner	Base colour	1st highlight	2nd highlight
Coat & breeches	Beige Brown (875) 80% + Cavalry Brown (982) 20%	Base colour 70% + Tan Yellow (912) 30%	1st highlight 70% + Tan Yellow (912) 30%
Belts	Hull Red (985)	Saddle Brown (940)	Saddle Brown (940) 70% + Tan Yellow (912) 30%

(Figure 125)

(Figure 126)

(Figure 127)

(Figure 128)

Artilleryman with portfire

This soldier wears a buff coat, a very popular semi-rigid jacket used both as clothing and light armour, and reddish brown breeches (Figures 129-130). The base colours (Figure 131) will be Beige Brown (875) and Hull Red (985) respectively, progressively mixed with Tan Yellow (912) and Cavalry Brown (982) for the first highlight (Figure 132) and second highlight (Figures 133-134). The original figure's headgear was an English montero cap, which was out of place in the Thirty Years War European context, so the cap was easily swapped for a German-style morion helmet.

(Figure 129)

(Figure 130)

(Figure 131)

(Figure 132)

(Figure 133)

(Figure 134)

Artilleryman	Base colour	1st highlight	2nd highlight
Buff coat	Beige Brown (875)	Beige Brown (875) 70% + Tan Yellow (912) 30%	1st highlight 70% + Tan Yellow (912) 30%
Breeches	Hull Red (985)	Hull Red (985) 50% + Cavalry Brown (982) 50%	1st highlight 10% + Cavalry Brown (982) 90%
Boot-hose	Chocolate Brown (872)	Chocolate Brown (872) 50% + Beige Brown (875) 50%	1st highlight 10% + Beige Brown (875) 90% or plain Beige Brown (875)

Artilleryman with sponge staff and ramrod

The last two artillerymen are poor fellows who were in charge of the harder tasks, as their role is closer to a labourer than a gunner (Figures 135-136). To reflect their lowly rank the base colours (Figure 137) of both the waistcoat and the breeches of the first figure were mixed with a bit of grey to get a faded look, and White (951) was used in highlights (Figures 138-140) to strengthen this greyish effect.

(Figure 135)

(Figure 136)

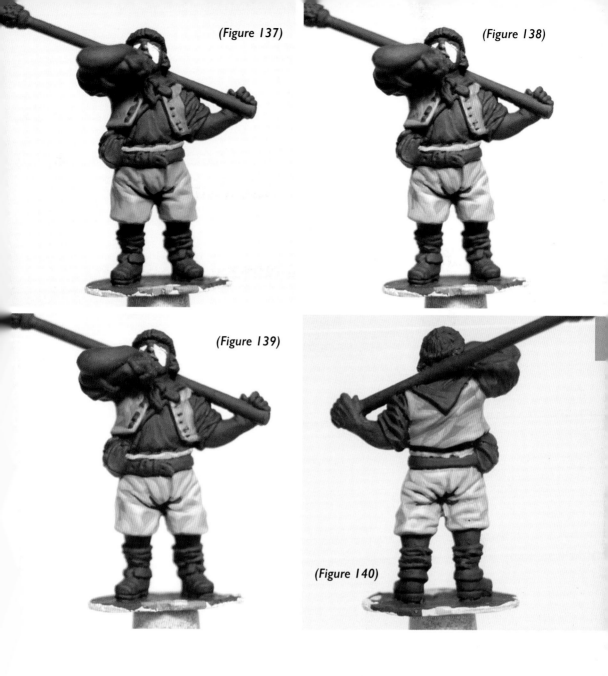

(Figure 137)

(Figure 138)

(Figure 139)

(Figure 140)

Artilleryman	Base colour	1st highlight	2nd highlight
Waistcoat	Chocolate Brown (872) 80% + Neutral Grey (992) 20%	Base colour 70% + White (951) 30%	1st highlight 70% + White (951) 30%
Breeches	Beige Brown (875) 90% + Neutral Grey (992) 10%	Base colour 70% + White (951) 30%	1st highlight 70% + White (951) 30%
Belt	Hull Red (985)	Saddle Brown (940)	Saddle Brown (940) 70% + Tan Yellow (912) 30%

Artilleryman with barrel

We'll take advantage of this figure to paint another two different colour combinations, a red leather waistcoat and dark greyish brown breeches (Figures 141-142). For the former I decided to mix the usual Hull Red (985) with Red Leather (818) to smooth it, but either Saddle Brown (940) or Mahogany Brown (846) would work as well as the base colour (Figure 143). We'll add more Red Leather (818) to the previous mix for the first highlight (Figure 144) and Tan Yellow (912) for the second highlight (Figures 145-146).

(Figure 142)

(Figure 141)

(Figure 143)

(Figure 144)

(Figure 145)

(Figure 146)

Artilleryman	Base colour	1st highlight	2nd highlight
Waistcoat	Hull Red (985) 80% + Red Leather (818) 20%	Base colour 50% + Red Leather (818) 50%	1st highlight 80% + Tan Yellow (912) 20%
Breeches	Chocolate Brown (872) 90% + Black (950) 10%	Base colour 80% + White (951) 20%	1st highlight 80% + White (951) 20%
Bag	Chocolate Brown (872)	Chocolate Brown (872) 80% + White (951) 20%	1st highlight 80% + White (951) 20%

(Figure 147)

(Figure 148)

(Figure 149)

(Figure 1

GUN AND EQUIPMENT

Besides the gun (Figure 147), this Warlord Games set came with a gunpowder barrel and an ammunition box, and this is perfect to show three different colour combinations to represent unpainted wood. Although all these pieces have relatively plain surfaces, I decided to paint two highlights using the drybrush technique. As mentioned earlier colours fade a little with this technique, so the contrast between base colour and highlights must be greater than with regular highlighting (Figures 148-151).

Regarding the metals, the technique I use to paint bronze guns is very easy, but involves more steps than usual, and requires some drying time in between steps. Citadel Colour references are going to be used as, in my

(Figure 151)

Wood	Base colour	1st highlight	2nd highlight
Gun carriage	Hull Red (985)	Mahogany Brown (846) *db*	Mahogany Brown (846) 70% + Tan Yellow (912) 30% *db*
Gunpowder barrel	Beige Brown (875)	Beige Brown (875) 50% + Tan Yellow (912) 50% *db*	Tan Yellow (912) *db*
Ammunition box	Chocolate Brown (872)	Chocolate Brown (872) 70% + White (951) 30% *db*	1st highlight 70% + White (951) 30% *db*

(Figure 152)

opinion, this company's metallic paints are superior to Vallejo's. I follow a five step process:

1. Base colour: Paint the gun barrel with several layers of watered down Citadel Shining Gold (61-63) to get a smooth result: we don't want a rough or lumpy finish! Repeat until the colour looks homogeneous and the primer cannot be seen. Paint the gun carriage's iron reinforcements (Figure 152).

(Figure 153)

(Figure 154)

2. Apply a wash either of a watered mix of Black (950) plus Hull Red (985) or any dark patina only on the muzzle, those parts of the barrel with some high relief (such as around the bands of the gun) and to the carriage's iron reinforcements (Figure 153). Let this dry (this won't take long if you gave a the gun a wash of watered down paint, but will take longer if you used a patina).

3. Repaint the upper parts of high relief, leaving the

(Figure 155)

dark wash/patina in the recesses. You have two options for the gun's muzzle: don't repaint it to leave a blackened effect for a well-used gun (as I've done), or repaint it for cleaner and brighter result (Figure 154)

4. Brass guns would loose their original brightness pretty quickly on campaign, so I varnish the barrel to give it a matt effect. Let this dry for a couple of hours or so (Figure 155)

5. Finally, give the barrel a slight drybrush of a lighter gilded colour such as Citadel Burnished Gold to get a vivid effect. A drybrush of Gunmetal Grey could be also applied to the reinforcements, although I decided not to do it as I like them just as they are: dark and matt cast iron (Figure 156).

Metals	Base colour	Wash	Repaint	Varnish	Drybrush
Bronze gun	Shining Gold (61-63)	Black (951) + Hull Brown (985) w or patina	Shining Gold (61-63)	Marabú's Mattlack	Burnished Gold (61-62) db
Iron fittings	Gunmetal Grey (863)	Watered Black (951) w or patina			Gunmetal Grey (863) db

(Figure 156)

9

Grey

Like brown, grey is a very useful colour that is easily mixed to get a wide variety of shades, from darker to lighter and from pure grey to brownish. Many military units chose grey for their uniforms, from English Civil War Scots to First Carlist War Carlists, and it's also a common colour for blankets, greatcoats, and other kit. However, the army chosen to show how to paint this peculiar colour was pretty evident: Perry Miniatures' American Civil War Confederates (Figure 157).

Unlike other colours you don't need to have a wide variety of greys. I do most of my painting with Neutral Grey (992), which can easily be darkened or lightened by adding black or white. An extra shade of a lighter grey (mainly to be used as base colour for whites) and a blue grey would be enough.

PAINTING TIP

(Figure 157)

PRIVATE IN SHELL JACKET

The shell jacket was an almost universal garment in Confederate armies by the mid-war, when early issue frock coats were worn out (and these jackets were cheaper to manufacture!). This soldier is relatively well equipped, wearing the grey shell jacket, regulation blue grey trousers and a forage cap as a headdress. However, instead of the usual black leather belts and cartridge box he has brown leather equipment. As you will see, adding some brown to the grey makes it look more realistic. For the trousers, I chose French Mirage Blue (900) as it's a bit lighter and more vivid than Grey Blue (943). However, if you don't want to buy both colours just use the Grey Blue (943) and mix it with black.

(Figure 158)

(Figure 159)

Private in shell jacket	Base colour	1st highlight	2nd highlight
Shell jacket & forage cap	Neutral Grey (992) 80% + Chocolate Brown (872) 20%	Base colour 80% + White (951) 20%	1st highlight 80% + White (951) 20%
Trousers	French Mirage Blue (900) 90% + Black (950) 10%	French Mirage Blue (900) 80% + White (951) 20%	1st highlight 70% + White (951) 30%
Belts & cartridge box	Hull Red (985)	Mahogany Brown (846)	Mahogany Brown (846) 70% + Tan Yellow (912) 30%
Bread bag	Black (951)	Black (951) 80% + White (951) 20%	1st highlight 80% + White (951) 20%

(Figure 160)

103

PRIVATE IN BATTLESHIRT

When shell jackets weren't available, grey shirts were customized as a substitute. This was very common at the beginning of the war. As the shirt was a thinner garment than the coat I decided to paint in a lighter colour, by not adding brown. On the other hand, for trousers and cap I used a darker version of the same grey.

Private in battleshirt	Base colour	1st highlight	2nd highlight
Battleshirt	Neutral Grey (992)	Neutral Grey (992) 70% + White (951) 30%	1st highlight 70% + White (951) 30%
Trousers & cap	Neutral Grey (992) 80% + Black (951) 20%	Base colour 80% + White (951) 20%	1st highlight 80% + White (951) 20%
Belts & cartridge box	Black (951)	Black (951) 70% + Mahogany Brown (846) 30%	1st highlight 70% + Mahogany Brown (846) 30%
Bread bag	Light Grey (990) 50% + Raw Sienna (113) 50%	Base colour 50% + White (951) 50%	1st highlight 50% + White (951) 50%

(Figure 161)

(Figure 162)

(Figure 163)

PRIVATE IN CIVILIAN SHIRT

Sometimes Confederate soldiers had to provide their own equipment. This private is wearing civilian clothes, from his shirt and trousers to his hat. Civilian shirts could be white, grey, red or checked: I've chosen the latter for this figure. For this kind of work I like to use a common base colour for the whole garment. After drawing black thin lines for the checks, highlights are added using different colours.

Private in civilian shirt	Base colour	1st highlight	2nd highlight
Shirt	Hull Red (985)	Mahogany Brown (846)/Cavalry Brown (982)	Chosen 1st highlight 70% + Tan Yellow (912) 30%
Trousers	Chocolate Brown (872)	Chocolate Brown (872) 80% + White (951) 20%	1st highlight 80% + White (951) 20%
Hat	Neutral Grey (992) 50% + Raw Sienna (113) 50%	Base colour 70% + White (951) 30%	1st highlight 70% + White (951) 30%
Bread bag	Light Grey (990) 50% + Raw Sienna (113) 50%	Base colour 50% + White (951) 50%	1st highlight 50% + White (951) 50%

(Figure 164)   *(Figure 165)*   *(Figure 166)*

OFFICER IN FROCK COAT

When grey dye was not available, the Confederate army started to use a butternut colour, especially for officers' uniforms. Although this is not properly grey, I think a butternut colour scheme is useful to include for Confederate figures. In this case it is a frock coat faced in the sky blue characteristic of the infantry. For the trousers, this officer wears the regulation blue grey, this time painted using the Grey Blue (943) instead of the French Mirage Blue (900) to achieve a more vivid shade. For gold embroidery see the previous chapter.

Officer in frock coat	Base colour	1st highlight	2nd highlight
Frock coat	Beige Brown (875) 80% + Hull Red (985) 20%	Base colour 70% + Tan Yellow (912) 30%	1st highlight 70% + Tan Yellow (912) 30%
Facings	Grey Blue (943) 70% + Prussian Blue (965) 30%	Base colour 70% + White (951) 30%	1st highlight 70% + White (951) 30%
Trousers	Grey Blue (943) 80% + Black (951) 20%	Grey Blue (943)	Grey Blue (943) 70% + White (951) 30%
Belts	Black (951)	Black (951) 80% + White (951) 20%	1st highlight 80% + White (951) 20%

(Figure 167)

(Figure 168)

(Figure 169)

(Figure 170)

10

Green

Green is a very common military colour, especially since the First World War. Prior to that, many units also wore green, including eighteenth-century Russian armies, Napoleonic chasseurs and British Riflemen and American Civil War sharpshooters. However, in order to show as many shades as possible using only a few figures, I've decided to paint three *Lord of the Rings* Rangers of Minas Tirith made by Games Workshop (Figure 170).

> *As we'll see, green is a very versatile colour. From the same base colour we can make multiple shades depending on the colour chosen for the highlights. Most of the time I use a sand colour for the highlights – Tan Yellow (912), Iraqi Sand (819) or Buff (976) – and this results in a very realistic finish. However, we could also mix with white (to get a paler or pastel effect), with yellow (for a vivid finish) or even with flesh-coloured paint.*

PAINTING TIP

(Figure 171)

(Figure 172)

RANGER ONE

Let's start with two versions of the classic Military Green (975). For the cloak we will paint a 'Napoleonic' green, mixing the Military Green (975) with Black (950) for the base colour and adding a sandy colour for the highlights. This also works well for British Riflemen, Napoleonic Russians and Bergan Sharpshooters. However, for the tunic we'll mix the Military Green (975) with an Olive Green (850) for the highlights, creating a very different final result. Military Green (975) is a very versatile colour; besides the combinations mentioned above, it marries well with white, yellow or flesh.

Ranger One	Base colour	1st highlight	2nd highlight
Cloak	Military Green (975) 80% + Black (950) 20%	Base colour 80% + Tan Yellow (912) 20%	1st highlight 80% + Tan Yellow (912) 20%
Tunic	Military Green (975)	Military Green (975) 50% + Medium Olive (850) 50%	Medium Olive (850)
Trousers	Chocolate Brown (872)	Chocolate Brown (872) 50% + Beige Brown (875) 50%	1st highlight 10% + Beige Brown (875) 90%
Armour & shoes	Beige Brown (875)	Beige Brown (875) 70% + Tan Yellow (912) 30%	Beige Brown (875) 70% + Tan Yellow (912) 30%
Leather bracelets, belts & quiver	Hull Red (985)	Mahogany Brown (846)	Mahogany Brown (846) 70% + Tan Yellow (912) 30%

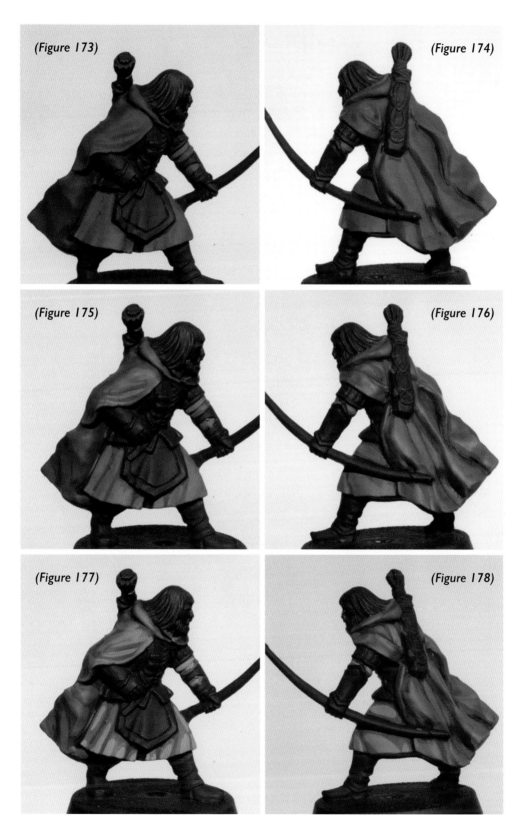

(Figure 173) (Figure 174)

(Figure 175) (Figure 176)

(Figure 177) (Figure 178)

RANGER TWO

Is this a Ranger or Vasily Zaytsev? He looks like a Second World War Russian sniper, right? For this figure we'll paint a variety of khakis that are very useful for a variety of twentieth-century forces, not just Russians. Khaki works well with sandy colours, but may also be mixed with white.

(Figure 179)

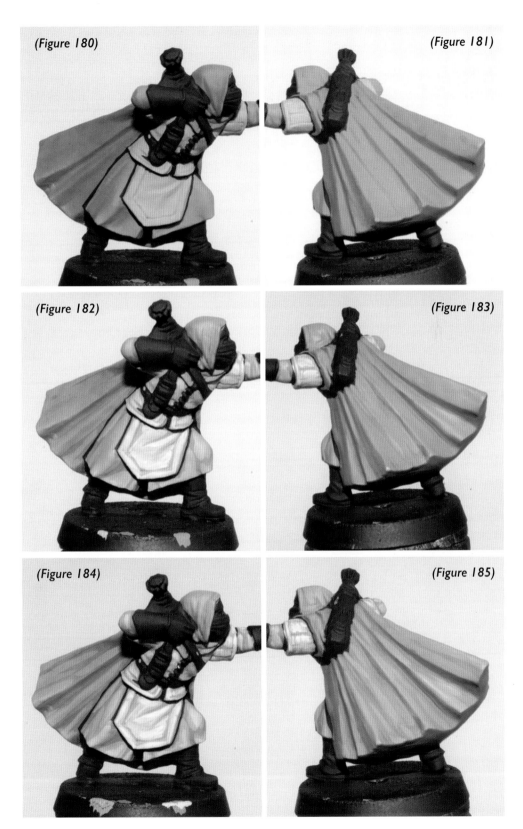

(Figure 180) (Figure 181)

(Figure 182) (Figure 183)

(Figure 184) (Figure 185)

113

Ranger Two	Base colour	1st highlight	2nd highlight
Cloak	Russian Uniform (924)	Russian Uniform (924) 70% + Tan Yellow (912) 30%	1st highlight 70% + Tan Yellow (912) 30%
Tunic	Khaki Grey (880)	Khaki Grey (880) 70% + Tan Yellow (912) 30%	1st highlight 70% + Tan Yellow (912) 30%
Armour	Khaki (988)	Khaki (988) 70% + White (951) 20%	1st highlight 70% + White (951) 30%
Trousers	Military Green (975)	Military Green (975) 70% + Tan Yellow (912) 30%	1st highlight 70% + Tan Yellow (912) 30%
Shoes	Chocolate Brown (872)	Chocolate Brown (872) 50% + Beige Brown (875) 50%	1st highlight 10% + Beige Brown (875) 90%
Leather bracelets, belts & quiver	Hull Red (985)	Mahogany Brown (846)	Mahogany Brown (846) 70% + Tan Yellow (912) 30%

(Figure 186)

RANGER THREE

If Ranger Two looked like a Russian sniper, this one could be Major König as both his cloak and tunic resemble a Second World War German uniform. As before, these colours marry well with sandy colours or white.

(Figure 187)

(Figure 188)

(Figure 189)

(Figure 190)

(Figure 191)

(Figure 192)

(Figure 193)

(Figure 194)

Ranger Three	Base colour	1st highlight	2nd highlight
Cloak	German Uniform (920)	German Uniform (920) 70% + White (951) 30%	1st highlight 70% + White (951) 30%
Tunic	Dark Green (893)	Dark Green (893) 70% + Tan Yellow (912) 30%	1st highlight 70% + Tan Yellow (912) 30%
Armour	Chocolate Brown (872)	Chocolate Brown (872) 50% + Beige Brown (875) 50%	1st highlight 10% + Beige Brown (875) 90%
Shoes & scarf	Military Green (975)	Military Green (975) 70% + Tan Yellow (912) 30%	1st highlight 70% + Tan Yellow (912) 30%
Leather bracelets, belts & quiver	Hull Red (985)	Mahogany Brown (846)	Mahogany Brown (846) 70% + Tan Yellow (912) 30%

11

Metals

We'll finish this section on colours by looking at how to paint metals. So far I've shown different approaches for doing so, from armour to cannons (for example, a wash was used for Jon Snow's chainmail and a patina for the Thirty Years War gun). All these techniques are valid for every type of armour, and patinas are especially useful as this gives an appearance of dirt or rust. However, this chapter focuses on metallic finishes in their own right.

STEP BY STEP

To demonstrate painting metals I decided to use a Warlord Games Early Imperial Roman centurion (Figures 195-196). As always we'll glue it to an empty bottle and prime it in black before doing anything else.

(Figure 195)

(Figure 196)

(Figure 197)

(Figure 198)

1. First of all we'll paint the chainmail, using the black of the undercoat as a base colour and painting two consecutive highlights with Gunmetal Grey (863) and Chainmail (61-56) using the drybrush technique. We'll also paint the crest now using the drybrush technique (Figures 197-198).

PAINTING TIP

Drybrushing can be a hard to control technique, especially when painting large areas such as the chainmail in this example, where leather reinforcements, belts and even pteryges may be accidentally painted. So it is wise to do this dirty business before painting any other areas, when it's still easy to correct.

2. Right after the drybrush, we'll repaint in black all the areas we painted accidentally, and then paint the base colours of the helmets, greaves, belt, gladius and other

metal parts using Gunmetal Grey (863) plus Black (951) for iron, and Brass (801) plus Black (951) for bronze (Figure 199).

3. Now we'll paint the first highlight using Chainmail (61-56) for iron and Shining Gold (61-63) for bronze. Note that the brass helmet decoration will be painted over the same base colour we used for the iron; there is no need to paint individual base colours to these tiny areas (Figure 200). If you are not a fan of shiny metallic finishes, you can do what we did with the Thirty Years War gun (varnishing the metallic parts of the figure to present a matt finish).

(Figure 199)

(Figure 200)

4. Finally, we'll paint the second highlight: just some minor brushstrokes using Mithril Silver (61-55) for iron and Burnished Gold (61-62) for bronze. If you intend to varnish your figures to protect the painting, save this highlighting until you've varnished, otherwise the varnish will dull down all the shining metalwork.

Roman centurion	Base colour	1st highlight	2nd highlight
Chainmail	Black (951)	Gunmetal Grey (863) db	Chainmail (61-56) db
Iron items	Gunmetal Grey (863) 80% + Black (951) 20%	Chainmail (61-56)	Mithril Silver (61-55)
Bronze items	Brass (801) 80%+ Black (951) 20%	Shining Gold (61-63)	Burnished Gold (61-62)
Crest & tunic	Cavalry Brown (982)	Cavalry Brown (982) + Red (947)	Red (947) 90% + Scarlet (817) 10%
Pteryges, armour leather reinforcements & crest base	Chocolate Brown (872)	Chocolate Brown 50% (872) + Beige Brown (875) 50%	Beige Brown (875)
Pteryges' fringes	Beige Brown (875)	Raw Sienna (113)	Yellow Ochre (913)
Gladius grip	Beige Brown (875)	Raw Sienna (113)	
Gladius scabbard	Chocolate Brown (872)	Chocolate Brown 80% (872) + White (951) 20%	1st highlight 80% + White (951) 20%
Gladius belt	Hull Red (985) Mahogany Brown (846)		
Celtic shield (on the ground)	Beige Brown (875)	Beige Brown (875) 50% + Yellow Ochre (913) 50%	1st highlight 50% + Yellow Ochre (913) 50%

PART THREE

THEMES

(Figure 201)

(Figure 202)

12

Flesh

Painting flesh is no different to painting any other colour, although the two most important considerations are which colour combinations we should use and where exactly to apply the brushstrokes. The latter is the biggest challenge when painting naked humans, as muscle reliefs are not always as evident as with cloth or armour. As usual, this problem is solved by a combination of common sense, intuition and, of course, experience.

Although there are many colour combinations you could use to paint Caucasian skin, I mainly use Light Brown (929) or Orange Brown (981) for the base colour – both are quite similar – either straight from the pot or mixed with a pinch of Hull Red (985) for a bronzed skin, and either Sunny Skintone (845) or Flat Flesh (955) – also very similar– for the highlights. If you don't want to mix paints you could use Beige Brown (875) as the base colour and a mix of Light Brown/Orange and Sunny Skintone/Flat Flesh for the highlights. We'll devote the step by step to painting Caucasian skin as it's most common in miniature painting, but we'll also pay attention to other skin colours in this chapter. No matter what skin tone you're painting, I suggest reducing the contrast (especially on plainer surfaces) and in some cases increasing the number of highlights.

LEONIDAS

As a starting point we'll use Tale of War's Leonidas miniature, based on Frank Miller's *300* fictional character (Figure 201-202). With these well-defined muscles, I guess we'll have no problems figuring where to paint the highlights!

1. Assuming that a Spartan who wanders around half

naked under the scorching Greek sun is going to be well tanned, we'll add a generous amount of Hull Red (985) to the Light Brown (929) for the base colour (Figure 203).

2. For the highlights, given the size of the figure (generously larger than the typical 28mm) and the volume of the musculature, I decided to paint three highlights instead of the usual two, reducing the contrast between them (Figures 204-205). Regarding the colour combination for highlights, we could progressively add just Sunny Skintone (845) to the base colour, or supplement it with a bit of Light Brown (929). The final highlight (Figure 206) would be either a mix of the second plus Sunny Skintone or just Sunny Skintone, depending on the previous highlight's contrast and the progression of the mix.

Leonidas	Base colour	1st highlight	2nd highlight	3rd highlight
Skin	Light Brown (929) 80% + Hull Red (985) 20%	Base colour 70% + Sunny Skintone (845) 20% + Light Brown (929) 10%	1st highlight 70% + Sunny Skintone (845) 30%	2nd highlight 10% + Sunny Skintone (845) 90% or just Sunny Skintone (845)
Cloak	Cavalry Brown (982) 80% + Hull Red (985) 20%	Base colour 70% + Red (947) 30%	1st highlight 70% + Red (947) 30%	2nd highlight 80% + Iraqi Sand (819) 20%
Bronze	Brass (801) 80% + Black (950) 20%	Base colour 80% + Brass (801) 20%	Brass (801)	
Wood (shield & spear)	Chocolate Brown (872)	Chocolate Brown (872) 80% + White (951) 20%	1st highlight 80% + White (951) 20%	
Leather	Saddle Brown (949) 80% + Black (950) 20%	Base colour 10% + Saddle Brown (949) 90%	Saddle Brown (949)	

(Figure 203)

(Figure 204)

(Figure 205)

(Figure 206)

SKIN TONE AND VOLUME

Following on from the Leonidas step by step, let's explore different examples where both the colour combinations and the volume of the figure vary substantially.

Medium Caucasian

This Warlord Games' Celtic fanatic warrior is similar in terms of musculature to Leonidas, but I decided to paint him in a lighter tone, more suitable for a less-suntanned Gaul. No Hull Red (985) was added to the Light Brown (929) for the base colour. Alternatively, we could use Beige Brown (875) as a base colour (but not for the highlights). The contrast between highlights will be a bit higher than those for Leonidas as we'll use just two highlights.

Celtic fanatic (Figures 207-208)	Base Colour	1st highlight	2nd highlight
Skin	Light Brown (929)	Light Brown (929) 50% + Sunny Skintone (845) 50%	1st highlight 10% + Sunny Skintone (845) 90% or just Sunny Skintone (845)
Belt	Chocolate Brown (872)	Chocolate Brown (872) 50% + Beige Brown (875) 50%	Beige Brown (875)
Sword & scabbard	Chainmail (61-56) 80% + Black (950) 20%	Chainmail (61-56)	

(Figure 207)   (Figure 208)

Daenerys Stormborn will serve as an example for lighter shades of Caucasian skin. This very detailed and delicate Dark Sword figure doesn't have the exaggerate volume and muscles of the previous two examples, so the contrast between highlights needs to be considerably smoother.

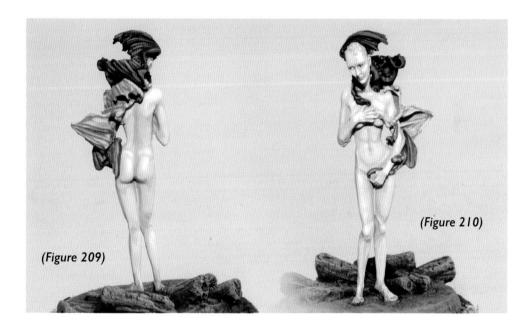

(Figure 210)

(Figure 209)

Daenerys Stormborn (Figures 209-210)	Base colour	1st highlight	2nd highlight
Skin	Light Brown (929) 60% + Sunny Skintone (845) 40%	Base colour 10% + Sunny Skintone (845) 90% or just Sunny Skintone (845)	Sunny Skintone (845) 90% + White (951) 10%
Viserion	Beige Brown (875)	Beige Brown (875) 50% + Yellow Ochre (913) 50%	Yellow Ochre (913)
Rhaegal	Military Green (975)	Military Green (975) 50% + Medium Olive (850) 50%	Medium Olive (850)
Drogon	Black (950)	Black (950) 80% + Iraqi Sand (819) 20%	1st highlight 80% + Iraqi Sand (819) 20%

Using the colour combination used for Leonidas, we'll just change Light Brown (929) for Beige Brown (875) both in the base colour and highlights. The Perry Miniatures' plastic Mahdist Ansar used here is painted with Beige Brown (875) as the only base colour, but alternatively this could be mixed with Hull Red (985) to get darker shades and give variety to your army. As with Daenerys Stormborn, when he's not battling the British army this fellow doesn't spend his free time at the gym, so watch the contrast!

(Figure 211)   *(Figure 212)*

Ansar (Figures 211-212)	Base colour	1st highlight	2nd highlight
Skin	Beige Brown (875) + Hull Red (985)	Base colour 80% + Sunny Skintone (845) 20%	1st highlight 80% + Sunny Skintone (845) 20%
Robes	Light Grey (990) 50% + Raw Sienna (113) 50%	Base colour 50% + White (951) 50%	1st highlight 50% + White (951) 50%
Belt & scabbard	Hull Red (985)	Hull Red (985) 50% + Cavalry Brown (982) 50%	Cavalry Brown (982)

Although multiple combinations are possible – with Black (950) or Chocolate Brown (872) as base colours – I used my favourite mix to paint this Empress/Warlord plastic Zulu warrior. This involves a change of colours: Hull Red (985) will play the role of Light Brown (929) as the predominant base colour paint, Black (950) will be used in the same way as previously the Hull Red (985) in order to get a darker base colour, and Light Brown (929) will be used for the highlights instead of Sunny Skintone (845).

(Figure 214)

(Figure 213)

Zulu warrior (Figures 213-214)	Base colour	1st highlight	2nd highlight
Skin	Hull Red (985) + Black (950)	Base colour 70% + Light Brown (929) 30%	1st highlight 70% + Light Brown (929) 30%
Cloth	Beige Brown (875)	Beige Brown (875) 60% + Iraqi Sand (819) 40%	1st highlight 60% + Iraqi Sand (819) 40%
Furs	Chocolate Brown (872)	Beige Brown (875)	(Spots) Black (950)

Rorke's Drift, Empress Miniatures, 28 mm.

13

Faces

In many cases the face is the most important part of the figure and, instinctively, the first thing we look at when we admire a model. Thus, although there are many aspects in common with the previous chapter devoted to painting skin, I've decided to devote a whole chapter to painting faces in order to give it the importance that, in my opinion, it deserves.

There are two different approaches to the painting of faces, depending on what overall look you require: the unit as a whole, depersonalizing individual figures; or miniature by miniature, reinforcing their individuality. It's not a matter of quality, but of concept.

For a less personalized style you can paint as described in the step by steps, but ignore those details that could personalize your figure (including the eyes). For a more individual style, the goal is to personalize as much as possible every single miniature. I prefer the latter style, and that's what I focus on in this chapter.

To explain the painting process I use, I've decided to paint three different Perry Miniatures' heads from their 40mm Peninsular War range (most of the miniatures come with several heads to choose, so I have piles of spare ones lying around). Regardless of their larger size, the same technique applies to regular 28mm faces but as these heads are a bit larger, they'll allow me to show every step in detail.

The order in which we have to paint the different elements is very important, and this is the procedure I always follow:

1. Base colour
2. Eyes
3. First highlight
4. Mouth and lower lip
5. Second highlight
6. Hair, moustaches, teeth, and other detail

(Figure 215)

(Figure 216)

(Figure 217)

(Figure 218)

As usual, glue the heads to empty bottles of paint or any other support to avoid touching the pieces during painting. Prime them in white using a spray and *except for the face itself* paint all over in black with a brush. The base colour will cover better over white and extra layers of paint would ruin the fine detail of a face, so it's better to avoid that.

FRENCH FUSILIER

1. As we have seen in the previous chapter on painting skin, we'll use the medium Caucasian colour combination for this first figure, so the base colour will be either Light Brown (929) or Orange Brown (981). The colour should be slightly watered down, but not too much or we'll need to give it two coats (Figure 215).

2. Right after the base colour we'll paint the eyes. Many people prefer to paint them as the very last step, when the rest of the face is finished. However, painting eyes is problematic and, even if you are very confident and experienced, it's easy to do it wrong at the first attempt: if the face is already painted, that would ruin part of an already complete paint job. On the other hand, if we paint the eyes now, we could easily correct them if something goes wrong. To paint the eyes, first paint the eyeball with white (Figure 216) and next add a black 'T' to represent the pupil and the upper eyelash (Figure 217). There is no need to paint all your eyes looking to the front: you could easily change the expression of your figure just by painting the pupils to the right or to the left of the eyeball (both pupils looking the same way, of course!). Now it's time to correct any mistakes with the base colour.

3. For the first highlight we'll mix the base colour with either Sunny Skintone (845) or Flat Flesh (955), about 50% of each. The painting process will be split into two steps. In the first one we'll paint what I like to call 'points of reference': the smaller areas such as eyelids and bags under the eyes, the space between the eyebrows and

(Figure 219)

besides the eyes ('crow's feet') and the upper lip (Figure 218). As with the eyes, any failed brushstroke could be corrected now before moving on to paint the bigger areas (Figure 219).

4. Paint the mouth in Hull Red (985) and the lower lip in a soft pinky colour such as Old Rose (944) or Salmon Rose (835). If you don't like pink for the lips, paint them the same colour as you used for the face's first highlight (Figure 220).

5. For the second highlight, we'll add more Sunny Skintone (845) or Flat Flesh (955) to the previous mix or use one of them straight from the pot, depending on the degree of contrast we're after. If we covered almost all the face surface with the first highlight, we'll paint just those parts of the bigger areas we want to project (Figure 221).

6. Finally, we will paint the chestnut hair. For the hair, a base colour – Chocolate Brown (872) – plus one highlight is enough in most cases. As it's a small surface drybrushing would be too messy, so it's easier (and safer) to paint the highlight by adding thin lines of the chosen colour, in this case Beige Brown (875). Finally, we'll paint the shako, the coat's collar, and other details (Figure 222).

(Figure 220)

(Figure 221)

(Figure 222)

French fusilier	Base colour	1st highlight	2nd highlight
Face	Light Brown (929)	Light Brown (929) 50% + Sunny Skintone (845) 50%	1st highlight 10% + Sunny Skintone (845) 90%
Hair	Chocolate Brown (872)	Beige Brown (875)	
Shako cover	Light Grey (990) 50% + Raw Sienna (113) 50%	Base colour 50% + White (951) 50%	1st highlight 50% + White (951) 50%
Collar	Cavalry Brown (982)	Cavalry Brown (982) 50% + Red (947) 50%	Red (947)
Collar piping	Light Grey (990)	White (951)	

(Figure 223)

(Figure 224)

BRITISH LINE INFANTRYMAN

1. In this case I wanted to use a lighter base colour, so I mixed Light Brown (929) with Flat Flesh (955). Regarding the eyes, note that the pupils were painted looking to his right (Figure 223).

2. For the first highlight I added extra Flat Flesh (955) to the base colour. I wanted to represent a younger chap, so I painted only small bags around the eyes, no crow's feet and linked the upper lip with the cheeks (Figure 224).

3. As I used a lighter base colour than usual, the contrast between it and the first highlight is very subtle, so I decided to reinforce some lines of expression using the lining technique (Figure 225) in this case adding lines of a mix of Light Brown (929) with a bit of Hull Red (985).

British line infantryman	Base colour	1st highlight	2nd highlight
Face	Light Brown (929) 70% + Sunny Skintone (845) 30%	Base colour 10% + Sunny Skintone (845) 90% *or just* Sunny Skintone (845)	Sunny Skintone (845) 70% + White (951) 30%
Face lining	Light Brown (929) 80% + Hull Red (985) 20%		
Hair	Beige Brown (875)	Yellow Ochre (913)	
Shako	Black (959)	Black (959) 80% + Neutral Grey (992) 20%	Base colour 80% + Neutral Grey (992) 20%
Shako plate	Shining Gold (61-63) 80% + Black (959) 20%	Shining Gold (61-63)	
Collar	Raw Sienna (113)	Raw Sienna (113) 50% + Iraqi Sand (819) 50%	Base colour 10% + Iraqi Sand (819) 90%
Collar piping	Light Grey (990)	White (951)	

4. The mouth and lower lip were painted, as before (Figure 226).

5. The second highlight was added (Figure 227) as before but using Flat Flesh (955) mixed with White (951).

6. The blonde hair was painted with Beige Brown (875) as the base colour and Yellow Ochre (913) for the highlight. Shako, collar, and other details were finished as before (Figure 228).

(Figure 225)

(Figure 226)

(Figure 227)

(Figure 228)

CATALAN GUERRILLERO

1. A darker base colour would better suit this hardened guerrillero, so we could mix Light Brown (929) plus Hull Red (985), or just Beige Brown (875). This will serve as the base colour for both the skin and the five o'clock shadow (described below). As for the eyes, note that he is looking to his left (Figure 229).

2. The first highlight of the skin will be painted with a mix of Light Brown (929) and Sunny Skintone (845). The painting areas are more or less similar to the French fusilier with the exception of the nasal bridge, here painted in two parts (like a broken nose). Regarding the five o'clock shadow, the first highlight will be painted using a combination of Beige Brown (875) and Sunny Skintone (845). If you want to simulate a heavier beard, use White (951) instead of Sunny Skintone (845) – the final effect will be greyish – or add some Neutral Grey (992) to the base colour (Figure 230).

Catalan guerrillero	Base colour	1st highlight	2nd highlight
Face	Beige Brown (875)	Light Brown (929) 70% + Sunny Skintone (845) 30%	1st highlight 20% + Sunny Skintone (845) 80%
Five o'clock shadow	Beige Brown (875)	Beige Brown (875) + Sunny Skintone (845)	1st highlight + Sunny Skintone (845)
Hair	Black (950)	Chocolate Brown (872)	
Grey hairs	Neutral Grey (992)	Sky Grey (989)	
Collar	Chocolate Brown (872)	Chocolate Brown (872) 50% + Beige Brown (875) 50%	Beige Brown (875)
Barretina	Cavalry Brown (982)	Cavalry Brown (982) 50% + Red (947) 50%	Red (947)

3. Paint the mouth and lower lip, as before but using the mix for the skin's first highlight (Figure 231).

4. Add the second highlights to the skin and five o'clock shadow, in both cases, by adding more Sunny Skintone (845) to their respective first highlight mixes (Figure 232).

(Figure 229)

5. The dark brown hair will be painted with Black (950) as the base colour and Chocolate Brown (872) for the highlight. Some grey hairs in the sideburns will add even more character to our miniature. The combination of greys would be darker or lighter, depending on the colour of the hair. Here we use Neutral Grey (992) for the base colour and Sky Grey (989) for the highlight. His barretina (Catalan cap), collar, and other details are finalized as before (Figure 233).

(Figure 230)

(Figure 231)

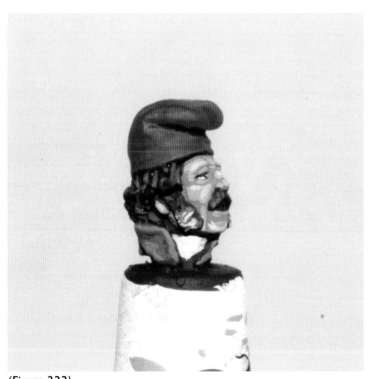

(Figure 233)

(Figure 232)

FACE PAINTING COLOUR CHARTS

Caucasian	Base colour	1st highlight	2nd highlight
Light Caucasian	Light Brown (929) + Sunny Skintone (845)	Base colour + Sunny Skintone (845) or just Sunny Skintone (845)	Sunny Skintone (845) + White (951)
Medium Caucasian	Light Brown (929)	Light Brown (929) + Sunny Skintone (845)	1st highlight + Sunny Skintone (845)
Dark Caucasian	Light Brown (929) + Hull Red (985) or Beige Brown (875)	Light Brown (929) + Sunny Skintone (845)	1st highlight + Sunny Skintone (845)
Mouth line	Hull Red (985)		
Lower lip	Old Rose (944) or as 1st Highlight		
Five o'clock shadow	Beige Brown (875)	Beige Brown (875) + Sunny Skintone (845)	1st highlight + Sunny Skintone (845)

Non-Caucasian	Base colour	1st highlight	2nd highlight
Arab/North African	Beige Brown (875) + Hull Red (985)	Beige Brown (875) + Sunny Skintone (845)	1st highlight + Sunny Skintone (845)
Black	Hull Red (985) + Black (950)	Hull Red (985) + Light Brown (929)	1st highlight + Light Brown (929)
Mouth line	Hull Red (985) or Black (950)		
Lower lip	as 1st highlight		

Hair	Base colour	1st highlight
Black hair	Black (950)	Black (950) + Neutral Grey (992)
Dark brown hair	Black (950)	Chocolate Brown (872)
Chestnut hair	Chocolate Brown (872)	Beige Brown (875)
Blonde hair	Beige Brown (875)	Yellow Ochre (913)
Ginger hair	Mahogany Brown (846)	Light Brown (929)
Dark grey hair	Dark Grey (994)	Neutral Grey (992)
Light grey hair	Neutral Grey (992)	Sky Grey (989)
White hair	Light Grey (990)	White (951)

14

Horses

Painting horses is easier than most people think and doesn't require any different techniques. However, there are two main differences from painting human figures. The first is that the surfaces are larger and plainer; due to this, we'll increase the number of highlights from two to three and reduce our usual degree of contrast between each highlight to create a more realistic finish. The second difference, and this is the big one, is … what colours should we use? Painting horsehair, the colour of which is often irregular and full of spots, dapples and different types of markings, is a real challenge. So developing good colour combinations is the key.

I'm by no means an expert on horses, and I apologize for any technical mistake I make about terminology: like most people, I've seen many horses with my own eyes (usually with a cop sitting astride it!) but never considered them in any greater detail. However, when I started to paint miniatures professionally I started to read and collect pictures of horses in order to develop practical colour combinations for my miniature equines that represent actual breeds of horses as realistically as possible. So, the terminology of this chapter could be simplistic and full of errors for an expert, but it's the practical outcome of years of practice and experimentation from the point of view of a miniatures painter.

EQUESTRIAN DEFINITIONS

Lets start explaining some useful concepts:

Coat: This is the colour of hair on the horse.

Points: The tail, the mane, some lower legs, and the points and the tips of the ears.

Skin: Seen where the hair is thinner (for example, on the nose, around the eyes, inside the ears, between the legs).

Markings: All horses have markings on their faces and legs of different shapes and sizes. Face markings could be a small star between the eyes, a stripe or a blaze running all the face down to the muzzle, the whole muzzle or just the lips and, in some cases, almost the whole face. Leg markings are of varied length: starting from the hoof, from shorter to longer we have coronet (around the hoof), pastern (up to the ankle), sock (mid lower leg) and stocking (up to the knee). Markings are always white.

NAPOLEONIC HORSES

The colour combinations described in this chapter represent modern breeds of horses, like those employed during the Napoleonic Wars (my examples use Perry Miniatures' British mounts).

As a general rule, leaving aside white and grey horses (which may be either heavy or light), heavy horses tend to have darker coloured coats and light horses tend to have lighter coloured coats. Some regiments regulated the colour of their mounts, either by squadrons or choosing a unique colour for the whole unit (such as the greys of the famous Scots Greys), although obviously that was impossible to maintain on campaign. Finally, it was a common practice (although not universal) to mount the trumpeters on white or grey horses.

STEP BY STEP

For this chapter's step by step I decided to use the horse type I paint more often: the red bay. Except in very special cases, I always assemble as many pieces as possible (including mounting riders on their horses) before starting to paint. I do this for a couple of reasons: first of all, I hate handling already painted figures, especially using glue on them; and gluing unpainted pieces together (bare metal to bare metal) is stronger than gluing painted bits (paint to paint). Once the rider, a British general in this case, was glued to the horse, both pieces were attached to an empty bottle of paint and primed in black. The rider was painted first, following the techniques described in the previous chapters, but now it's time to pay attention to his horse.

Coat

1. Using Hull Red (985) with some Black (950) we'll cover almost all the horse except for the tail, mane, socks and reins (Figure 234). There is no need to be especially careful to avoid these areas as they will be painted afterwards (just be sure not to ruin the rider!).

2. For the first highlight we'll add Cavalry Brown (982) to the base colour mix and paint over it, covering almost all the surface (Figure 235). This is the most difficult part: learning where to paint our brushstrokes and where to leave the previous coat.

3. For the second highlight we'll add more Cavalry Brown

(Figure 234)

(Figure 235)

(Figure 236)

(Figure 237)

(982) to the previous mix and repeat the process (Figure 236).

4. Finally, a third highlight will be painted, but this time adding not Cavalry Brown but Light Brown (929) to the previous mix. Watch this step, we don't want to cover too much of the previous highlight, just to paint minor touches to highlight the contours (Figure 237).

Points and markings

1. Once the coat is completed, we'll paint the base colour of the black points, the white marks and the nose. At this stage we'll paint the eyes too (Figure 238). Horses' eyes are not like human eyes: their pupils are bigger and get bigger when the horse is excited (such as during a charge). Thus, instead of painting the eyeball in white and the pupil in black, as we have seen in the chapter devoted to faces, we'll paint the whole eye in black, then paint just one small white 'corner' on top of the black pupil.

2. Points, markings and the nose receive two highlights, as do hooves (Figure 239). Hooves could be in different colours, from dark browns to light beige or bone, including grey. For the highlights, you could paint vertical stripes instead of the horizontal brushstrokes I did here. Mane and tail are highlighted using the drybrush technique. Belts and reins complete the piece (Figures 240-241).

(Figure 238)

(Figure 239)

(Figure 240)

(Figure 241)

Red bay	Base colour	1st highlight	2nd highlight	3rd highlight
Coat	Hull Red (985) 80% + Black (950) 20%	Base colour 80 + Cavalry Brown (982) 20%	1st highlight 80% + Cavalry Brown (982) 20%	2nd highlight 80% + Light Brown (929) 20%
Points	Black (950)	Black (950) 80% + Neutral Grey (992) 20%	1st highlight 80% + Neutral Grey (992) 20%	
Mane & tail	Black (950)	Black (950) 70% + Neutral Grey (992) 30% *db*	1st highlight 70% + Neutral Grey (992) 30% *db*	
Markings	Light Grey (990)	Light Grey (990) 50% + White (951) 50%	White (951)	
Nose	Beige Brown (875)	Light Brown (929) 70% + Flat Flesh (955) 30%	Flat Flesh (955)	
Hooves	Black (950)	Black (950) 70% + Mahogany Brown (846) 30%	1st highlight 70% + Mahogany Brown (846) 30%	

DAPPLED HORSES

Some horses – especially grey ones – have dapples on their hindquarters or all over their body. As we'll see in the following example, a Scot Greys officer, the painting process of a dappled horse is quite similar to other horses until the final highlight.

1. We'll use Light Grey (990) for the undercoat (Figure 242), and add White (951) for the first highlight (Figure 243) and the second highlight (Figure 244).

2. The third highlight, using just White (951), will be painted all over the horse's body except on the hindquarters, where instead of the usual brushstrokes we'll paint star-shaped spots (Figure 245). Whatever the colour of the horse, I always paint the dappling with the third highlight colour: using an even lighter colour creates too dazzling a look for me.

(Figure 242)

Figure 243)

(Figure 244)

(Figure 245)

Dappled	Base colour	1st highlight	2nd highlight	3rd highlight
Coat	Light Grey (990)	Light Grey (990) 70% + White (951) 30%	1st highlight 70% + White (951) 30%	2nd highlight 10% + White (951) 90%
Points	Black (950)	Black (950) 80% + Neutral Grey (992) 20%	1st highlight 80% + Neutral Grey (992) 20%	
Mane & tail	Black (950)	Black (950) 70% + Neutral Grey (992) 30% db	1st highlight 70% + Neutral Grey (992) 30% db	
Markings	Light Grey (990)	Light Grey (990) 50% + White (951) 50%	White (951)	
Hooves	Beige Brown (875)	Beige Brown (875) 50% + Tan Yellow (912) 50%	1st highlight 10% + Tan Yellow (912) 90%	

WHITE HORSES

Pure white horses are very uncommon. Actually, most of the horses that we recognize as white are actually grey. The main characteristics identifying a white horse are the points (which are white) and the skin (which is pink), while on grey horses both are black. There are also two peculiar horse colours called cremello and perlino, often wrongly considered albinos. They actually are chestnuts and bays with a double cream gene, so they are considered whites. Their coat is similar, though a perlino is a bit darker with reddish/orange points. Both have pink skin and blue eyes.

(Figure 246)

(Figure 247)

(Figure 248)

White (Figure 246)	Base colour	1st highlight	2nd highlight	3rd highlight
Coat	Sky Grey (989) or Light Grey (990)	Base colour + White (951)	1st highlight + White (951)	White (951)
Points	Light Grey (990)	Base colour + White (951)	1st highlight + White (951)	
Skin	Beige Brown (875)+ Old Rose (944)	1st highlight + Flat Flesh (955) or White (951)	1st highlight + Flat Flesh (955) or White (951)	

Perlino (Figure 248)	Base colour	1st highlight	2nd highlight	3rd highlight
Coat	Raw Sienna (113) + White (951)	Base colour + White (951)	1st highlight + White (951)	2nd highlight + White (951)
Points	Mahogany Brown (846) + Light Brown (929)	Base colour + White (951)	1st highlight + White (951)	
Skin	Beige Brown (875) + Old Rose (944)	Base colour + Flat Flesh (955) or White (951)	1st highlight + Flat Flesh (955) or White (951)	

Cremello (Figure 247)	Base colour	1st highlight	2nd highlight	3rd highlight
Coat	Light Grey (990) + Raw Sienna (113)	Base colour + White (951)	1st highlight + White (951)	2nd highlight + White (951)
Points	Light Grey (990) + Raw Sienna (113)	Base colour + White (951)	1st highlight + White (951)	
Skin	Beige Brown (875)+ Old Rose (944)	Base colour + Flat Flesh (955) or White (951)	1st highlight + Flat Flesh (955) or White (951)	

GREY HORSES

Greys are horses with black skin and a mixture of white, grey and black hair. So their coats can be extremely varied and they often have mottled coats. Moreover, coats lighten with age, so dark grey horses such as steel grey turn into light or dapple greys. Finally, there are also grey horses with brown genes, producing grey-rose coloured coats. Their points are dark and tails and manes could be either black or coloured as the coat.

(Figure 249)

Light grey (Figure 249)	Base colour	1st highlight	2nd highlight	3rd highlight
Coat	Light Grey (990)	Light Grey (990) + White (951)	1st highlight + White (951)	2nd highlight + White (951)
Points	Black (950)	Black (950) + Neutral Grey (992)	1st highlight + Neutral Grey (992)	
Skin	Black (950)	Black (950) + Neutral Grey (992)	1st highlight + Neutral Grey (992)	

(Figure 251)

(Figure 250)

Dapple grey (Figure 250)	Base colour	1st highlight	2nd highlight	3rd highlight
Coat	Neutral Grey (992) + Black (950)	Base colour + White (951)	1st highlight + White (951)	2nd highlight + White (951)
Points	Black (950)	Black (950) + Neutral Grey (992)	1st highlight + Neutral Grey (992)	
Skin	Black (950)	Black (950) + Neutral Grey (992)	1st highlight + Neutral Grey (992)	

Steel grey (Figure 251)	Base colour	1st highlight	2nd highlight	3rd highlight
Coat	Black (950) + Neutral Grey (992)	Base colour + White (951)	1st highlight + White (951)	2nd highlight + White (951)
Points	Black (950)	Black (950) + Neutral Grey (992)	1st highlight + Neutral Grey (992)	
Skin	Black (950)	Black (950) + Neutral Grey (992)	1st highlight + Neutral Grey (992)	

Rose grey (Figure 252)	Base colour	1st highlight	2nd highlight	3rd highlight
Coat	Neutral Grey (992) + Raw Sienna (113)	Base colour + White (951)	1st highlight + White (951)	2nd highlight + White (951)
Points	Black (950)	Black (950) + Neutral Grey (992)	1st highlight + Neutral Grey (992)	
Skin	Black (950)	Black (950) + Neutral Grey (992)	1st highlight + Neutral Grey (992)	

(Figure 252)

LIGHT BROWN HORSES

There are three types of horses in this category: dun, buckskin and palomino. They all have a coat colour that varies from a very light sandy yellow to beige and reddish browns. The main difference between them is the points: dun's points are a darker version of the colour of the coat (or black), buckskin's are always black and palomino's are cream, off-white or golden yellow. Dun horses keep some primitive features such as a dorsal stripe and sometimes even 'zebra' markings, especially on their legs.

Light (Figure 253)	Base colour	1st highlight	2nd highlight	3rd highlight
Coat	Raw Sienna (113)	Raw Sienna (113) + Tan Yellow (912)	1st highlight + Tan Yellow (912)	2nd highlight + Tan Yellow (912)
Points (dun)	Raw Sienna (113)	Raw Sienna (113) + Tan Yellow (912)	1st highlight + Tan Yellow (912)	
Points (buckskin)	Black (950)	Black (950) + Neutral Grey (992)	1st highlight + Neutral Grey (992)	
Points (palomino)	Light Grey (990) + Raw Sienna (113)	Base colour + White (951)	1st highlight + White (951)	

(Figure 253)

(Figure 254)

Bay (Figure 254)	Base colour	1st highlight	2nd highlight	3rd highlight
Coat	Beige Brown (875)	Beige Brown (875) + Flat Flesh (955)	1st highlight + Flat Flesh (955)	2nd highlight + Flat Flesh (955)
Points (dun)	Beige Brown (875)	Beige Brown (875) + Flat Flesh (955)	1st highlight + Flat Flesh (955)	
Points (buckskin)	Black (950)	Black (950) + Neutral Grey (992)	1st highlight + Neutral Grey (992)	
Points (palomino)	Light Grey (990) + Raw Sienna (113)	Base colour + White (951)	1st highlight + White (951)	

(Figure 255)

Red (Figure 255)	Base colour	1st highlight	2nd highlight	3rd highlight
Coat	Beige Brown (875) + Cavalry Brown (982)	Base colour + Flat Flesh (955)	1st highlight + Flat Flesh (955)	2nd highlight + Flat Flesh (955)
Points (dun)	Beige Brown (875) + Cavalry Brown (982)	Base colour + Flat Flesh (955)	1st highlight + Flat Flesh (955)	
Points (buckskin)	Black (950)	Black (950) + Neutral Grey (992)	1st highlight + Neutral Grey (992)	
Points (palomino)	Light Grey (990) + Raw Sienna (113)	Base colour + White (951)	1st highlight + White (951)	

DARK BROWN HORSES

Two types of horses represent the dark brown colour spectrum: bays and chestnuts. Their variations offer us a good spectrum of colours; depending on the genes, bay and chestnut coats can vary from a saddle or reddish brown to a very dark brown, almost black. In fact, dark

Light chestnut (Figure 256)	Base colour	1st highlight	2nd highlight	3rd highlight
Coat	Mahogany Brown (846) + Black (950)	Base colour + Mahogany Brown (846)	1st highlight + Mahogany Brown (846)	2nd highlight + Tan yellow (912)
Points (bay)	Black (950)	Black (950) + Neutral Grey (992)	1st highlight + Neutral Grey (992)	
Points (light chestnut)	Mahogany Brown (846) + Black (950)	Base colour + Mahogany Brown (846)	1st highlight + Mahogany Brown (846)	
Points (flaxen chestnut)	Light Grey (990) + Raw Sienna (113)	Base colour + White (951)	1st highlight + White (951)	

(Figure 256)

156

bays and liver chestnuts could be mistaken for black horses. Again, the main difference between them is the points: bay's points are black, while chestnut's are of the same colour as the coat. There is a chestnut variation called flaxen, whose points are off-white/creamy like the palomino.

(Figure 257)

Red chestnut (Figure 257)	Base colour	1st highlight	2nd highlight	3rd highlight
Coat	Hull Red (985) + Black (950)	Base colour + Cavalry Brown (982)	1st highlight + Cavalry Brown (982)	2nd highlight + Light Brown (929)
Points (red bay)	Black (950)	Black (950) + Neutral Grey (992)	1st highlight + Neutral Grey (992)	
Points (red chestnut)	Hull Red (985) + Black (950)	Base colour + Cavalry Brown (982)	1st highlight + Cavalry Brown (982)	
Points (red flaxen chestnut)	Light Grey (990) + Raw Sienna (113)	Base colour + White (951)	1st highlight + White (951)	

(Figure 258)

Dark chestnut (Figure 258)	Base colour	1st highlight	2nd highlight	3rd highlight
Coat	Black (950)	Black (950) + Mahogany Brown (846)	1st highlight + Mahogany Brown (846)	2nd highlight + Mahogany Brown (846)
Points (dark bay)	Black (950)	Black (950) + Neutral Grey (992)	1st highlight + Neutral Grey (992)	
Points (liver chestnut)	Black (950)	Black (950) + Mahogany Brown (846)	1st highlight + Mahogany Brown (846)	
Skin	Black (950)	Black (950) + Mahogany Brown (846)		

158

BLACK HORSES

Unlike dark bays and liver chestnut, pure black horses have no sign of brown on them at all, not even in their mane or tail.

Black (Figure 259)	Base colour	1st highlight	2nd highlight	3rd highlight
Coat	Black (950)	Black (950) + Neutral Grey (992)	1st highlight + Neutral Grey (992)	2nd highlight + Neutral Grey (992)
Points	Black (950)	Black (950) + Neutral Grey (992)	1st highlight + Neutral Grey (992)	
Skin	Black (950)	Black (950) + Neutral Grey (992)	1st highlight + Neutral Grey (992)	

(Figure 259)

PINTO HORSES

Although mostly associated with Western movies, pinto horses were quite popular in Europe until the nineteenth century, when their use for military purposes declined due to the belief that they were weak animals. Obviously this is not the type of horse on which to mount an entire regiment, but a pinto can look nice for a light cavalry officer or an ADC (Figure 260). Pintos haven't a unique coat colour as they are not a specific breed of horse, so almost any of the coat colour combinations described previously could be useful for a pinto. Although it's a bit complicated, to simplify we can distinguish three types of pintos:

Tobiano: Smooth shaped white spots cover the loins, while the coat colour covers one or both flanks, neck and chest. All four legs have white markings, as well as the face.

Overo: We could say that overo is the opposite to the tobiano as the white spots are irregular shaped and the back of the horse and one or more of the legs are coloured like the coat, without white markings. An overo's face tends to be 'bald' (wholly covered by white markings).

Tovero: A mix of tobiano and overo ... who dares to paint one.

(Figure 260)

Shields

Many companies sell transfers for shields, and their quality has dramatically improved in recent years from the basic plain decals of the past to the awesome, life-like transfers produced by Little Big Men Studios. Even so, I'm one of the endangered species of painter who still likes to hand paint shields. In fact, painting shields is a part of the painting process that I really enjoy because working on a flat surface feels different to the other parts of a figure.

(Figure 261)

PAINTING TIP

As a general rule, plain surfaces require very smooth contrasts, so be careful with the mixtures you make for your highlights. I also recommend diluting the paint more than usual to avoid lumps or brush marks on the finished surface.

STEP BY STEP

We'll learn the standard step-by-step painting procedure with a Warlord Games Early Imperial Roman plastic shield. As usual, we need to attach the shield to something that allows us to hold it while we are painting without having to touch the shield itself. If painting a number of shields all at one time, the best option is to hammer a line of headless nails into a strip of wood and glue the shields to the nails by the shield's grip. In this case, we're working on an individual shield, so we'll glue it to an old brush handle and undercoat it white. To give it some character, make some cuts with a modelling knife to represent battle scars.

(Figure 262)

1. First of all, we have to paint the background, including the base colour and highlights, before painting any design on it (Figure 261). For this we'll use Cavalry Brown (982) as the base colour, progressively mixed with Red (947) for the two highlights (the last one is almost pure red).

2. Now we'll start to paint the shield design, starting with

(Figure 263)

(Figure 264)

the points of reference, (a concept explained in the chapter devoted to faces). As this is a symmetrical design, we'll mark in black the rivets of the shield's metal reinforcements. This will help us as a reference to paint the first part of our design. With Beige Brown (875) we'll paint the main (Figure 262) traces of the spine (from the middle of the shield boss to the central upper and lower rivets); the wings (from the corners of the boss to the rivets in the corners of the reinforcement); the blocks (between the sides of the boss and the lateral rivets).

Once these main traces are done, we'll complete the wings (Figure 263) with three extra lines (for a total of four) and paint the lightning bolts (Figure 264) with Sky Grey (989).

3. Next we add the highlights, two for the spine, wings and blocks using Raw Sienna (113) for the first highlight (Figure 265) and Yellow Ochre (913) for the second (Figure 266), and one for the lightning bolts in White (951).

4. Finally, we'll paint the metals, first lining every metallic area with black and then painting a base colour: Chainmail (61-56) plus Black (950) for the boss, Shining Gold (61-63) plus Black (951) for the edge's reinforcement, and one highlight of Chainmail (61-56) and Shining Gold (61-63) respectively. A Hull Red (985) lining is also painted at the shield cuts (Figure 267).

(Figure 265)

(Figure 266)

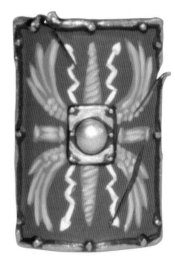

(Figure 267)

Roman shield	Base colour	1st highlight	2nd highlight
Background	Cavalry Brown (982)	Cavalry Brown (982) 50% + Red (947) 50%	1st highlight 10% + Red (947) 90%
Spine, wings & blocks	Beige Brown (875)	Raw Sienna (113)	Yellow Ochre (913)
Lightning bolts	Sky Grey (989)	White (951)	
Iron boss	Chainmail (61-56) 80% + Black (950) 20%	Chainmail (61-56)	
Brass reinforcement	Shining Gold (61-63) 80% + Black (951) 20%	Shining Gold (61-63)	

Late Republican Romans, Wargames Foundry, 28 mm.

PATINAS

Patinas are used to darken folds and project volumes, so theoretically they do not seem to be a good technique for painting flat shield surfaces. Also, the painting of shields requires a smooth degree of contrast, which a patina does not create. However, the use of patinas is a good technique for painting shields as it helps to disguise any mistakes or irregularities of painting. The Wargames Foundry Late Roman shields we'll use in the following example demonstrate the effect of patinas on different colours. As usual with patinas, the regular process step by step will differ:

1. Instead of painting the whole background, both base colour and highlights, and then the design, we'll paint the base colours for both the background and the design (Figures 268-269).

(Figure 268)

2. Apply the patina, removing any accumulation with the brush. Don't use a very dark patina, a medium or light one is much more suitable (Figures 270-271).

3. Paint two highlights to the background and the design (Figures 272-273).

(Figure 269)

(Figure 270)

Round shield	Base colour	1st highlight	2nd highlight
Background	Cavalry Brown (982)	Cavalry Brown (982) 60% + Red (947) 40%	1st highlight 10% + Red (947) 90%
Yellow edge	Light Brown (929)	Light Brown (929) 60% + Flat Yellow (953) 40%	Flat Yellow (953)
White edge	Light Grey (990)	Sky Grey (989)	White (951)
Eagle	Black (950)	Black (950) 80% + Neutral Grey (992) 20%	
Iron boss	Gunmetal Grey (863)	Chainmail (61-56)	

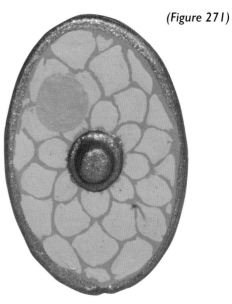

(Figure 271)

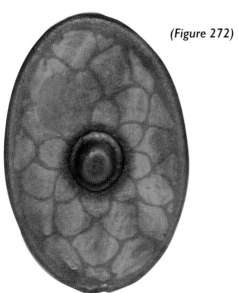

(Figure 272)

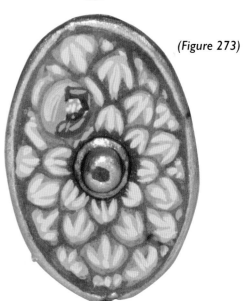

(Figure 273)

Oval shield	Base colour	1st highlight	2nd highlight
Background/ petals	Beige Brown (875)/Raw Sienna (113)	Raw Sienna (113)	Yellow Ochre (913)
Blue circle	Blue Grey (943) 70% + Prussian Blue (965) 30%	Base colour 80% + White (951) 20%	1st highlight 80% + White (951) 20%
Portrait face		Light Brown (929)	Flat Flesh (955)
Portrait clothes		Violet (960)	Blue Violet (811)
Brass edge & boss	Brass (801)	Shining Gold (61-63)	

16

Flags

There are countless companies selling paper flags that are easy to assemble, cheap, of high quality and realistic (such as GMB or Adolfo Ramos). However, I am sure you'll agree with me that hand-painted flags (Figure 274) beat paper ones. I am not going to lie to you: making a flag is difficult. It requires a lot of time and patience and requires you to know how to draw as well as how to paint. But more positively, you will notice a huge difference when you see your units finished off with a magnificent flag that you painted yourself. So, if you have time, I encourage you to try.

For homemade flags we could use paper (as thin as possible), but tin paper is much better as it's flexible and malleable, even when painted. Tin paper is easy to find in a large ironmonger's and it is quite cheap (the type usually sold in specialized hobby stores is very expensive and is no different to that available in an ironmonger's).

As always we need to fix whatever we are going to paint to a surface to make the painting process easier. Take a block of wood and drill a series of holes (depending on how many flags you are going to paint at the same time) in it as far part as possible with a 0.7mm bit. We'll mount the flags on metal rods and fit them into these holes, so it is important that the rods fit snugly because this will make the painting and drying process much easier. Being a French flag (the pole of which will be crowned by an eagle), we'll use steel wire to glue the flags to; the wire allows us to hold the flag without any difficulty while we are painting. Metal spears with their heads removed also make good flag staffs.

(Figure 274)

(Figure 275)

(Figure 276)

(Figure 277)

STEP BY STEP

1. Some people calculate the flag's dimensions, mark these onto the tin paper with a ruler and then cut them out. This takes quite some time to do so I recommend buying paper flags and using them as a template for the dimensions, design and colours. You should always cut your flags out a tad bigger than the template because the lining will eat up some space and because you will have to attach one of the sides to the steel pole. What I do is add 1mm on three sides and 5mm on the side where the steel pole is going to be, to make a sleeve. Once you have cut the piece out of tin paper, you should roll the side that is going to be attached using the steel pole to help you. Then all you have to do is stick the pole into the sleeve you made on the side of the tin paper. To finish fixing it, lower the flag to the middle of the staff, apply quick-drying glue to the top and then quickly slide the flag back up, leaving only the tip of the staff sticking out (Figure 275). Lastly, apply a layer of quick-drying glue to the flag sleeve to fill the joint. It is important that you use a good quick-drying glue because, if not, it will

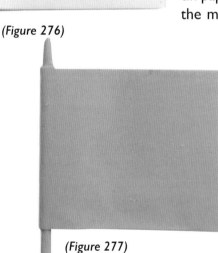

(Figure 278)

crystallize in the joint and form lumps that are difficult to paint.

2. Once the glue has dried completely, you should apply a white spray undercoat (Figure 276). Use white because the colours of this flag are light. You must use a spray primer: if you don't, the paint will chip when you go to fold the flag into shape.

3. After the primer has dried, apply two coats of diluted Light Grey (990) with a brush (Figure 277). It is important that there are no lumps or brush marks because this will make the flag look very artificial.

(Figure 279)

4. Now you should start to apply the colours of the flag's 'diamond'(Figure 278). Mark the four corners of the diamond and paint the red areas with a mixture of Cavalry Brown (982) with a bit of Black (950). For the blue parts, mix Prussian Blue (965) with Black (950). Do not worry if it is not perfect because you will be able to touch up the centre with Light Grey (990) once these areas are dry. For the edges (the flag's fringe), you should use Beige Brown (875). If you see that the paint has not taken well you will have to apply another coat.

5. When the paint is dry and after you have made sure that you have applied enough paint, paint the lining (Figure 279). In this particular case, you only have to be careful when lining the outside part that simulates the fringe. If the lines of the diamond area are too thick it does not matter because later you add golden laurels on top of them.

(Figure 280)

At this stage, decide which type of folds the flag is going to have. This will depend on the pose of the figures in the unit you are going to use the flags with. I have chosen a simple and standard fold so that it is easier to see (Figure 280). Make sure you clean your hands well so that you do not leave any smudges or shiny marks, and then pick up the flag and bend it. If you have any difficulties, you can use a cylindrical surface, like a brush handle, to help you. You should not fold it completely: froll it just

(Figure 281)

enough so that you can see exactly where you are going to add highlights (if you fold it too much you will not be able to paint on it anymore!) and do it gently to avoid the paint cracking. The final folds will be made at the end of the process.

(Figure 282)

6. After you have made the folds, begin to add the highlights on the highest areas of them (Figure 281). Applying the first highlights is the most difficult since these define the flag's depth and volume. Make sure that all the highlights are consistent with the folds that you have made. For the first highlight of white, mix Light Grey (990) and White (951). Make sure you dilute the paint well so that there are no lumps. I recommend applying two coats because these colours tend to be difficult, especially when diluted. For the red parts, apply a mixture of Cavalry Brown (982) and Red (947). For the blue areas, use Prussian Blue (965).

7. Now that the hardest part of highlighting is finished, you need to add two more highlights, gradually reducing the surface where you apply the paint. So, the third highlight should only be applied to the highest areas of the flag's folds.

(Figure 283)

For reds: For the second highlight, add more Red (947) to the previous mix. Red (947) with a bit of Scarlet (817) is used for the third highlight. You should add two coats of this red so that it is strong and stands out.

For blues: Apply the second highlight with a mixture of Prussian Blue (965) and White (951), adding more white to the mix for the third highlight.

For white: On the diamond, add more White (951) to the previous mix for the second highlight and paint two coats of pure White (990) for the third highlight.

8. You have now completed the standard flag painting

process, so now move on to the writing step. Since this flag has a lot of written decoration on it and it would be practically impossible to outline each and every one of the tiny laurels (Figure 282), you should instead paint the area Black (950). Make the drawing a bit bigger than it should be so that when you paint the colours of the gold threads on top a small edge is left exposed, marking and outlining the drawing (Figure 283).

The most important detail of the drawing is that the letters fit and that the laurel wreaths do not end up being too small or too big. To prevent these difficult to correct mistakes, use visual reference points (the paper flag used for the template will help you here). In this particular case, the most difficult part is making sure that all the letters fit well in the centre. I painted the line in the centre first as it is the longest and this acted as a reference for the top and bottom lines. To write the letters and to paint the laurels I used a brand new thin brush.

9. Now that the most difficult part is done, the only thing left for you to do is to start to add the gold thread effect. Use the same mixture that you applied to the edges of the flag: Beige Brown (875). This mixture should be applied very carefully with a thin brush over the letters and the decoration that you previously marked with black. Try to leave the black outline whenever you can.

10. Once the flag's lines are perfectly defined, all you have to do is add the final details. To obtain the gold thread effect, paint the highest areas of the decoration and the letters (following the highlights you added in the other colours). For this, use Raw Sienna (113) or a mixture of Beige Brown (875) and Yellow Ochre (913). You will use this same mixture to imitate the flag's fringe. Paint small perpendicular lines on the corresponding edge and then connect these with parallel lines. A second highlight will be painted using Yellow Ochre (913). To finish it off, add a few touches of Burnished Gold (61-62) to different areas of the gold thread so that it shines.

The flag is finished! Now you have to fold it to get a

prettier and more realistic effect. Once you have folded it, add the 'eagle' to the top of the tip of the staff that you left hanging out of the top of the flag. When you have completed all of the steps, cut the steel pole with scissors and glue it to your figure; paint the flagstaff after you have glued it to the figure (to prevent the paint from chipping when you handle it). As French flag staffs were blue, I have applied the same mixtures I used for the blue parts of the flag.

Lastly, if there is any glue residue on the joint of the figure, you should varnish it so that you get a totally matt finish. As you can see, the result is spectacular (Figure 284).

(Figure 284)

Flag	Base Colour	1st highlight	2nd highlight	3rd highlight
White	Light Grey (990)	Light Grey (990) 70% + White (951) 30%	1st highlight 70% + White (951) 30%	White (951)
Blue	Prussian Blue (965) 80% + Black (950) 20%	Prussian Blue (965)	Prussian Blue (965) 80% + White (951) 20%	2nd highlight 80% + White (951) 20%
Red	Cavalry Brown (982) 90% + Black (950) 10%	Cavalry Brown (982) 60% + Red (947) 40%	1st highlight 20% + Red (947) 80%	Red (947) 90% + Scarlet (817) 10%
Fringe & embroidery	Beige Brown (875)	Raw Sienna (113)	Yellow Ochre (913)	Burnished Gold (61-62)

17

Camouflage

If you're collecting armies for the Second World War or modern conflicts, sooner or later you will be confronted with painting camouflage. But don't worry, it's much easier than it looks: the complicated part is to choose the right colours.

The variety of camouflage is huge, from the complicated patterns of the Waffen SS to the relatively simple scheme for Soviet scouts. However, I use the same technique to paint them all. First of all, we must identify the predominant colour in the uniform. Depending on the camouflage pattern, this could be hard (British paratroopers, for example). This step is quite important as this is the colour we are going to use to paint the first stages of the uniform. Employing the usual technique, we'll paint a base colour plus two highlights. Once done, the camouflage will be painted over it (representing the shapes and spots of the respective pattern) using diluted colours (but not quite so watered as used for a wash). This way, the main colour and the camouflage spots merge better and the camouflage gains depth without the need for any highlight.

As I mentioned before, the difficult thing is to identify the right base colours to use according to the sources we have at hand. Most times I'll use illustrated uniform books (such as Osprey's publications) as a reference, but in some cases – especially for Modern conflicts – we have colour photos at our disposal. To translate real colours to miniatures will require a good eye, not only for the base colours but for the highlights too.

> *Always avoid strong colours and always mix the highlights with white or sand colours. It's a good idea to add a bit of black to the base colour to make greens and khakis even less colourful*
>
> PAINTING TIP

MODERN RUSSIANS

To demonstrate painting camouflage, I decided to use some fantastic Red Star Modern Russians for the war in Chechnya. The reason is evident: the Russians employed an enormous variety of camouflage (including privately purchased garments), from greens and browns to grey and blue urban camouflages, so we can try out many different patterns. If you see a bunch of soldiers from this conflict

Soldier 1 (Figures 285-286)	Base colour	1st highlight	2nd highlight	Camouflage
Uniform	Russian Uniform (924)	Russian Uniform (924) 70% + Iraqi Sand 30% (819)	1st highlight 70% + Iraqi Sand (819) 30%	
Armour	Raw Sienna (113) 80% + Hull Red (985) 20%	Base colour 80% + White (951) 20%	1st highlight 80% + White (951) 20%	Russian Uniform (924) & Beige Brown (875) 90% + Hull Red (985) 10%

(Figure 285)

(Figure 286)

all dressed in different uniforms, you can bet they are not Chechens but Russians! To crown it all, I painted not regular soldiers but tank riders to place on a ubiquitous BMP-2 infantry combat vehicle.

As the non-camouflage painting follows the same procedure explained many times before in this book, I'll just focus on the figures pre-camouflage and post-camouflage.

(Figure 287)   *(Figure 288)*

Soldier 2 (Figures 287-288)	Base colour	1st highlight	2nd highlight	Camouflage
Uniform	Raw Sienna (113) 80% + Hull Red (985) 20%	Base colour 80% + White (951) 20%	1st highlight 80% + White (951) 20%	Russian Uniform (924) & Beige Brown (875) 90% + Hull Red (985) 10% w
Armour	Russian Uniform (924)	Russian Uniform (924) 70% + Iraqi Sand 30% (819)	1st highlight 70% + Iraqi Sand (819) 30%	Military Green (975) & Chocolate Brown (872) w
Hat	Chocolate Brown (872)	Chocolate Brown (872) 80% + White (951) 20%	1st highlight 80% + White (951) 20%	Russian Uniform (924) w

(Figure 289)   (Figure 290)

Soldier 3 (Figures 289-290)	Base colour	1st highlight	2nd highlight	Camouflage
Uniform	Neutral Grey (992)	Neutral Grey (992) 70% + White (951) 30%	1st highlight 70% + White (951) 30%	Neutral Grey (992) + Black (951) & Black (951) + Neutral Grey (992) w
Armour	Dark Green (893)	Dark Green (893) 70% + Iraqi Sand (819) 30%	1st highlight 70% + Iraqi Sand (819) 30	

(Figure 291)   (Figure 292)

Soldier 4 (Figures 291-292)	Base colour	1st highlight	2nd highlight	Camouflage
Uniform	Khaki (988)	Khaki (988) 70% + Iraqi Sand (819) 30%	1st highlight 70% + Iraqi Sand (819) 30%	Beige Brown (875) & Russian Uniform (924) w
Armour	Russian Uniform (924)	Russian Uniform (924) 70% + Iraqi Sand 30% (819)	1st highlight 70% + Iraqi Sand (819) 30%	Military Green (975) & Chocolate Brown (872) w

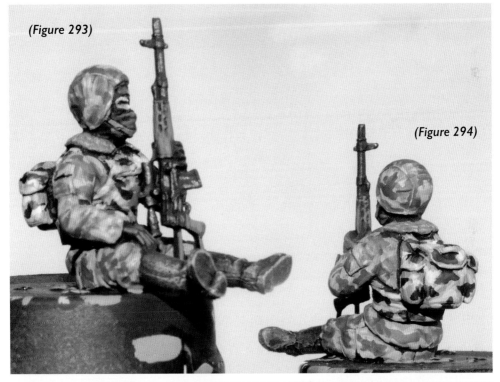

(Figure 293)

(Figure 294)

Soldier 5 (Figures 293-294)	Base colour	1st highlight	2nd highlight	Camouflage
Uniform	Dark Green (893)	Dark Green (893) 70% + Iraqi Sand (819) 30%	1st highlight 70% + Iraqi Sand (819) 30%	Military Green (975) & Chocolate Brown (872) w
Armour	Grey Blue (943) 70% + Prussian Blue (965) 30%	Base colour 70% + White (951) 30%	1st highlight 70% + White (951) 30%	Sky Grey (989) & Black (951) w

(Figure 295)

(Figure 296)

Soldier 6 (Figures 295-296)	Base colour	1st highlight	2nd Highlight	Camouflage
Uniform	Khaki (988)	Khaki (988) 70% + Iraqi Sand (819) 30%	1st highlight 70% + Iraqi Sand (819) 30%	Beige Brown (875) & Russian Uniform (924) w
Armour	Raw Sienna (113) 80% + Hull Red (985) 20%	Base colour 80% + White (951) 20%	1st highlight 80% + White (951) 20%	Beige Brown (875) 90% + Hull Red (985) 10% w

(Figure 297)

(Figure 298)

Soldier7 (Figures 297-298)	Base colour	1st highlight	2nd highlight	Camouflage
Uniform	Dark Green (893)	Dark Green (893) 70% + Iraqi Sand (819) 30%	1st highlight 70% + Iraqi Sand (819) 30%	Military Green (975) & Chocolate Brown (872) w
Armour	Dark Green (893)	Dark Green (893) 70% + Iraqi Sand (819) 30%	1st highlight 70% + Iraqi Sand (819) 30%	

Common Equipment	Base colour	1st highlight	2nd highlight
Fur lining & brown gloves	Chocolate Brown (872)	Chocolate Brown (872) 80% + White (951) 20%	1st highlight 80% + White (951) 20%
Black gloves	Black (950)	Black (950) 80% + Neutral Grey (992) 20%	1st highlight 80% + Neutral Grey (992) 20%
Helmet	Military Green (975) 80% + Black (950) 20%	Base colour 90% + White (951) 10%	
Gun metal	Black (950)	Black (950) 30% + Gunmetal Grey (863) 70%	
Small arms magazines	Hull Red (985) 80% + Red Leather (818) 20%	Red Leather (818)+	
Heavy weapon magazines	Military Green (975)	Gunmetal Grey (863)	
Boots	Black (950)	Chocolate Brown (872) *db*	Raw Sienna (113) *db*

BMP-2 carrying Russian troops, Chechen Wars. Resin vehicle by HLBS.

18

Basing

This important but overlooked element of miniatures painting is often regarded as a routine and even painstaking step for many modellers. However, like the frame of a masterpiece, basing is an integral part of our figure and is just as important as any other element of the piece. In fact, the smaller the scale of our figure the more relevant the terrain will be to the end result. Both experienced and not-so-experienced painters know that obtaining a top-notch paint job requires a considerable amount of time. So, why not invest a little bit more time on the figure's base to achieve a perfect finish?

BASE TYPES

First of all, we must decide which type of base we want to use for our figures. A wide assortment of ready-made bases are available, whose measurements normally fit the most popular rule sets. These bases tend to be made from plastic, although you can also find some made from cardboard or laser cut wood. If you don't like what's commercially available, you can make your own at home. The most common materials for doing this are cardboard, wood and plastic card since they are easy to work with; however, other materials – such as aluminium – have quite a few fans. Using a square, draw the bases you're going to need on the material you've chosen. The more you do in one sitting the better. This way you can plot your bases like a grid on the material to get the most efficient use out of it. If you opt for aluminium, you'll have to machine-cut it; in this case, it's a good idea to have the shop you buy it from do this for you.

The advantage of using plastic and aluminium is that

they will stay flat no matter what dimension you use and they will never warp. However, you have to be really careful with wood and cardboard because the glue or the moisture from the putty can warp them. However, contact glue, modelling putty and paint do adhere better to cardboard and wood. Plastic and aluminium usually need to be treated before use, scoring the surface with a knife or priming/varnishing the base (Figure 299).

(Figure 299)

Modelling Sand

This creates the easiest and quickest base you can build and will give you acceptable results.

A good number of different options of sand are available, as well as homemade alternatives. To get a variety of sizes and textures, I use a mixture of beach sand (washed and dried), fine modelling sand and fine gravel (Figure 300).

(Figure 300)

First glue the miniature to the base and, once the glue is dry, apply a coat of watered-down white glue to the base and cover it with sand (Figure 301). Shake the excess off and allow it to dry. This can take up to a couple of hours. If the coat of glue is too thick it will pull up at the sides as it dries and could warp a cardboard or wooden base. As the sand tends to be stored in a ziplock bag or a container, I recommend you pour it out onto a piece of paper to use. This way, after you've used what you need, you can lift the paper, make a cone shape and pour the excess back into the container.

(Figure 301)

Painting sand bases

1. Once the glue has dried, we'll use a round brush to paint the sand. Using Raw Sienna (113) we paint the edge of the base first. Use it as is: don't dilute it. This way we'll probably only need one coat. After that, we paint the sand the same colour. This time, though, we do want to water down the paint. By doing this, the sand absorbs the paint faster and shortens the process (Figure 302). Although acrylic paints dry fast, it will take a bit longer in this case since they've been watered down (approximately a half an hour).

2. When the undercoat is dry, we drybrush the entire surface with Buff (976). Use an old brush or a flat brush for this.

3. Lastly, we put some white glue in different areas of the stand and add some vegetation. You can use either static grass or flock, whatever suits your tastes. I usually use static grass for 28mm and flock for 15mm, but it also depends on what I'm painting.

(Figure 302)

The best way to do this is to put a good handful on the glue, pressing down with your finger or a tool. Then shake

(Figure 303)

off the excess (Figure 303). As with the sand, I recommend you use a piece of paper as a tray so that you can easily pour the excess back into its container after using it.

You can place the grass on your base either randomly or strategically. It can be used to conceal any flaws or ugly parts of the terrain (Figure 304): areas where the sand didn't stick well and has left bald spots, excessive height on the figure's metal base, supports to fix figures onto the base and so on (Figure 305).

Sand terrain	Base colour	1st highlight
Sand	Raw Sienna (113)	Buff (976) *db*

(Figure 304)

(Figure 305)

Modelling Putty

This type of basing is much more time consuming to make and paint than using modelling sand. However, the result is a lot more spectacular. First off, this terrain 'grows': the surface is elevated in contrast to a flat base on which the only vertical element was the figure itself. Adding trunks, rocks and field grass, the figure is accompanied and surrounded by other elements that rise from the surface; so, instead of having just a flat base and a mounted figure, we get a more harmonious and realistic appearance. In addition, the uneven texture allows us to work better with the paint and to obtain a greater variety of contrasts and shades.

Materials

You'll need DAS modelling putty for the base, and wire, wire cutters, an unwanted brush, scissors, a modelling scalpel or something similar, a toothbrush and static grass (Figure 306). The DAS putty is very easy to handle and is softened with water. It slowly dries when it comes into contact with the air. So, once you open the sealed pack, you must always close it as airtight as possible and store it in a cool place (the fridge is perfect).

(Figure 306)

(Figure 307)

(Figure 308)

(Figure 309)

(Figure 310)

(Figure 311)

1. Let's start by sculpting the different terrain elements. In this case, I've used a twisted trunk, a rock, two stratified stones and field grass. First we'll make the trunk with putty over a wire frame. We cut out two pieces of wire (Figure 307), bend them in half and twist them together until we've got the shape we want (Figure 308). Leaving one of the legs of the wire flat to fix to the base, we cover the structure with wet DAS putty and give it some texture. To imitate bark, we add lines lengthwise with the modelling scalpel or knife and a couple of holes (Figure 309). We can also hollow out one of the two ends of the trunk if desired. Once this is done, carefully pick it up, add a bit of glue to the legs and sink it into the putty on the base. For the rock, we make a ball out of the putty and glue it to the base. We can leave it round or use our fingers to make any shape we like. For the stratified stones, make two balls of putty – one of which is twice the size of the other – and glue them together on the base. Using our fingers to hold the stone down, we use our other hand to make cuts along one of the sides using the modelling knife (Figure 310).

2. Now we prepare a piece of DAS putty by wetting it and rolling out before putting it onto the base. Even though it's not strictly called for, it's a good idea to put a diluted coat of white glue over the entire base so that the putty adheres better. The layer of putty shouldn't be too thick (unless you need it to be for something specific). Here we want to use just enough so that we can add texture to it (Figure 311). While the putty is still fresh, we'll add the trunk, the rocks and, lastly, the field grass. Take the unwanted brush, grab a section of the hairs and use the scissors to cut them off. While still holding the tuft of hairs, put glue onto the bottom and press them down into the putty on the base. If the hairs are very stiff after being glued on, we can open them up with a knife (Figure 312).

(Figure 312)

3. After we've added all the terrain elements, we need to hide any glue that's showing and add some more texture to the base. To do this, we use a modelling scalpel or any other tool we have at hand. We can add cracks, footprints, grooves, etc., exaggerating or accentuating them all. Once that's done, we finish it off by adding texture with the toothbrush. Use it on the base terrain and the rocks: drag it, pressing hard or softly or combing the putty with it (Figure 313). Allow the putty to dry completely; this may take a couple of hours.

(Figure 313)

Painting putty bases

1. Paint the base with Raw Sienna (113), the trunk and rock with Chocolate Brown (872) and the stratified stones with Neutral Grey (992) and allow it to dry. We won't paint the field grass, but we do want to put a touch of diluted Sienna Brown (AD113) on the base so that the hairs absorb the paint from the bottom up to the tips (Figure 314).

2. Mix Chocolate Brown (872) with a tiny bit of Black (951); then water this down quite a bit to use it as a wash. Most of the mixture should be water since the objective is not to smear the whole base with it, but to create different nuances by allowing the paint to accumulate more or less in different areas. We apply this to the whole piece: the base, the rocks, the trunk and the base of the field grass. Let it dry (Figure 315).

3. With a flat brush, we drybrush the base again with Raw Sienna (113), the trunk and

(Figure 314)

(Figure 315)

(Figure 316)

the rock with Beige Brown (875) and the stratified stones with Light Grey (990) (Figure 316).

4. We drybrush the whole piece very lightly with Buff (976). As this last step covers all of the elements on the base, it pulls them all together and gives us an even finish (Figure 317).

5. Lastly, we add the grass as shown before (Figure 318). For a finishing touch, we add a light wash to an area on the rocks or stones with Military Green (975) to imitate moss (Figure 319).

(Figure 318)

(Figure 319)

Putty terrain	Base colour	Wash	1st highlight	2nd highlight
Sand	Raw Sienna (113)	Chocolate Brown (872) 90% + Black (959) 10% *w*	Raw Sienna (113) *db*	Buff (976) *db*
Grey rock	Neutral Grey (992)		Neutral Grey (992) *db*	
Brown rock	Chocolate Brown (872)		Beige Brown (875) *db*	
Trunk	Chocolate Brown (872)		Beige Brown (875) *db*	

Modelling sand and putty

This method combines the first two by adding quality touches from putty to the simplicity of the first in order to enrich your bases, elevate the terrain and integrate your figure.

(Figure 320)

Procedure

Decide what terrain elements to add to your base. Trunks, rocks and field grass will do just fine. Make a trunk and some rocks as shown in the previous section and fix them to the base with white glue. We also want to add a bit of putty for the brush hairs (field grass). We allow the putty and glue to dry (Figure 320). Once dry and solid, we apply white glue to the base and cover it with sand. We shake off the excess and allow it to dry (Figure 321).

(Figure 321)

Painting sand and putty bases

1. We'll paint the terrain exactly like the simple sand base. First of all we paint the base edge with non-diluted Raw Sienna (113), and then the sand with the same colour, but watered down (Figure 322).

(Figure 322)

(Figure 323)

2. Once dry, we'll paint the rocks with Neutral Grey (992) and the trunk with Chocolate Brown (872).

3. Then we drybrush the rocks with Light Grey (990) and the trunk with Sienna (113).

4. Finally, we drybrush the sand with Buff (976), giving a second light drybrush of this colour to the rocks and trunk, and glue the grass (Figure 323).

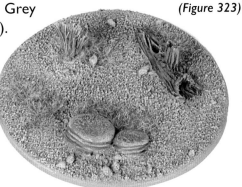

Sand & putty terrain	Base colour	1st highlight	2nd highlight
Sand	Raw Sienna (113)	Buff (976) *db*	
Grey rock	Neutral Grey (992)	Light Grey (990) *db*	Buff (976) *db*
Trunk	Chocolate Brown (872)	Raw Sienna (113) *db*	Buff (976) *db*

Textured pastes

There are several companies that sell textured pastes (such as Vandal's white paste and Vallejo's White Pumice). This is a very helpful product that brings with it a lot of advantages. Textured pastes allow us to get a quality and realistic terrain with the simplicity of the sand and the volume of the putty. Moreover, the paste can be easily dyed with acrylic paints, saving us a lot of time in the painting process. These pastes become really solid when they dry, so rocks and any other extra elements should be attached to it when it's fresh, and you don't even need to glue the figures to the base first! As you might imagine, this is the method I now use most often.

Procedure

1. As I decided to use an aluminium base, this needs some preparation before we get started. Attach the base to an empty can and prime it with a white spray. Then paint the edges with Sienna (113) and varnish it with a spray (Figure 324).

2. Now it's time to mount the figures. If you prefer to glue the figures to the base before working on it, spread the paste over the

(Figure 324)

(Figure 325)

190

(Figure 326)

(Figure 327)

base with a sculpting tool, also covering the miniatures bases. However, it's much faster if we use the paste as terrain and glue as well. First of all place the figures on the base to make your composition (Figure 325). Then remove the figures and spread the paste over the base (Figure 326), afterwards returning the figures and pressing them on hard (Figure 327). After a couple of minutes, cover the

(Figure 328)

bases of the miniatures with extra paste (or cover them later with grass or flock) and distribute some rocks over the fresh paste (Figure 328).

Painting paste bases

1. The painting of paste bases is similar to modelling putty ones, but saves the tedious first step of adding the base colour (as the paste was previously dyed). So, once the paste is completely dry – be patient, it could take a few hours – we'll give it a quick wash of diluted Chocolate Brown (872) (Figure 329).

2. Now we'll paint a general drybrush over the sand with Tan Yellow (912) and the rocks Neutral Grey (992) (Figure 330).

3. Finally, we'll give a second drybrush to the whole base, including rocks, with Buff (976) (Figure 331). Instead of using flock or grass, this base is completed gluing MiniNatur tufts (Figure 332).

Paste terrain	Wash	1st highlight	2nd highlight
Sand	Chocolate Brown (872)	Tan Yellow (912) *db*	Buff (976) *db*
Rocks		Neutral Grey (992) *db*	

(Figure 329)

(Figure 330)

(Figure 331)

(Figure 332)

19

Varnishing

Varnish is my personal nightmare. In fact, it's the only painting issue I don't have a completely satisfactory answer for. As I've mentioned before, I like a matt finish on my figures, and I haven't found completely matt varnish yet. However, there is something worse than a shiny matt finish, and this is 'whitening'. For several reasons, matt varnish may whiten when it dries, often in deeply sculpted areas. There is nothing more appalling than seeing long hours of hard work ruined because of the varnish, but I completely understand the necessity of protecting your figures, especially if you are a wargamer moving your models across the tabletop.

As a general rule, matt varnishes looks better but gloss ones give more protection to our figures. Added to this, solvent-based varnishes also protect better than acrylic ones.

SPRAY VARNISHING

This is the quickest and easiest way to protect your figures. Several companies such as Games Workshop and Army Painter offer good quality gloss, satin and matt varnishes in spray. However, even the matt ones are not completely matt. The final effect depends on the thickness of the coat applied. A thin coat looks better, but it doesn't provide much protection. Always remember to shake the can well before use.

BRUSH VARNISHING

Marabú Mattlack is my favourite varnish to brush onto models. It must be mixed well before use. I recommend you stir it with the handle of an old brush instead of shaking it (or even better, do both!). The whitening effect is generally due to a lack of mixing, so take this step very seriously: I usually count to one hundred when stirring, more if the can is new or if it has remained unused for a long time.

Once well mixed, I don't use the varnish straight from the pot. Instead, I put some varnish onto a plastic surface (an empty blister pack or a plastic spoon) and add some drops of turpentine or solvent to thin the thick varnish paste. Apply a thin coat of varnish to the figure and remove excessive accumulations.

As I explained in the chapter devoted to patinas, we can take out some of the medium before mixing the components of the varnish for an extra matt finish. By removing a third or fourth of the solvent, we'll increase the proportion of varnish in the container. I recommend doing this when you buy a new pot. The varnish settles on the bottom of the pot, perfectly separated from the solvent. However, this increases the chances of whitening, so stir well and add more turpentine or solvent to the mix once on the plastic surface.

DOUBLE VARNISH

This third option will offer you the benefits of both gloss (protection) and matt (realism) varnishes. The process is simple: first varnish the figure in gloss, let it dry overnight and then paint it matt. You can use brushed varnishing for both steps (some old-school painters use Humbrol enamel varnishes for that), but it's very time consuming waiting for it to dry. On the other hand you can do both steps with sprays, but as matt sprays are not completely matt, and given the indiscriminate nature of sprays, the second coat (matt) could miss parts previously varnished in gloss, leaving a patchy final effect.

I use an intermediate option: I apply the first gloss coat with a spray and, at least twelve hours later, add a second matt coat with Marabú. If the varnish is properly stirred and thinned with solvent or turpentine, the final effect should be mostly matt and as we are applying it with a brush we will cover the whole model without missing bits. However, once the matt varnish is dry, check the figure again just in case you have missed an area, and apply extra varnish accordingly.

First Carlist War (1833-1840), Perry Miniaturas, 28mm. Double varnished figures.

PART FOUR

OTHER SCALES

(Figure 333)

20

Larger Scales

Figures of sizes above 28mm, such as 54, 70 or 90mm, are not considered to be wargame miniatures but instead are collector's pieces. Usually displayed individually or in dioramas, as opposed to in massed units, the techniques used to paint these miniatures are completely different to those for wargame scales. However, there is a scale very popular in the USA that is progressively growing in popularity in Europe: 40mm. Halfway between 28mm and 54mm, a 40mm figure may be painted using the techniques and concepts shown in the previous chapters, with some minor variations. As a general rule, following my previous recommendations to paint bigger/plainer surfaces, we'll increase the number of highlights and reduce the contrast between them.

To show this technique we are going to paint a Perry Miniatures 40mm French dismounted hussar of the 4th Regiment, a truly beautiful and original piece that allows us to paint both a horse and a human figure (Figure 333). Before starting to paint, the figure requires some assembly. Any complex figure like this has several pieces that need to be glued, and sometimes the joints need to be filled with putty. Once assembled, the hussar and horse are glued to empty plastic containers and spray primed in white.

HUSSAR

After the white undercoat, we'll paint the hussar all over again with diluted black paint (this time using a brush), except the face as we don't want to lose it's fine detail under layers of paint. Once dry, check the figure for patches that the black paint didn't cover the first time.

1. As usual, we'll start by printing the predominant colours of the figure, in this case blue and red: the colours of the 4th. After the respective base colours (Figure 334) have dried, we'll paint three highlights over the blue (reducing the usual contrast) and two over the red (Figures 335-337).

(Figure 334)

(Figure 335)

(Figure 336)

(Figure 337)

2. Next, we paint the coat's yellow lace, using the base colour plus two highlights (Figures 338). Don't forget the colback bag piping!

(Figure 338)

(Figure 339)

(Figure 340)

3. We'll paint the skin in Beige Brown (875). Use the same painting procedure explained in the chapter devoted to faces, but increase the number of highlights to three and reduce the contrast between them. We'll start with the eyes (Figure 339), correcting any mistakes with the base colour before moving on. The next step, the first highlight, is split in two. First we'll paint the points of reference (Figure 340) that will help us to paint the rest of the face (Figure 341). We'll also paint the first highlight of the five o'clock shadow, and then the mouth and the lower lip (Figure 342). Finally, we'll paint the last highlights: a second and third highlight for the skin, a second highlight for the five o'clock shadow and one highlight for the lower lip (Figure 343). The head is completed by painting the hair and moustache, including some grey hairs in the sideburns of this hardened veteran (Figure 344).

4. Finally, paint the weapons, buttons, sabretache, trousers reinforcements, and other kit in the order you would prefer (Figures 345-346).

(Figure 341)

(Figure 342)

(Figure 343)

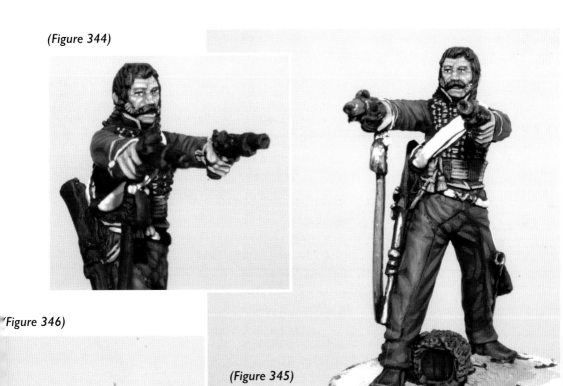

(Figure 344)

(Figure 345)

(Figure 346)

Hussar	Base colour	1st highlight	2nd highlight	3rd highlight
Dolman & trousers	Prussian Blue (965) 70% + Black (950) 30%	Base Colour 90% + Prussian Blue (965) 10%	1st highlight 90% + White (951) 10%	2nd highlight 90% + White (951) 10%
Facings	Cavalry Brown (982)	Cavalry Brown (982) 50% + Red (947) 50%	Red (947) 90% + Scarlet (817) 10%	
Lace	Beige Brown (875)	Beige Brown (875) 50% + Yellow Ochre (913) 50%	Yellow Ochre (913)	
Belts	Sky Grey (989)	Sky Grey (989) 50% + White (951) 50%	White (951)	
Face	Beige Brown (875)	Light Brown (929) 70% + Sunny Skintone (845) 30%	1st highlight 50% + Sunny Skintone (845) 50%	Sunny Skintone (845)
Five o'clock shadow	Beige Brown (875)	Beige Brown (875) 70% + Sunny Skintone (845) 30%	1st highlight 70% + Sunny Skintone (845) 30%	
Lower lip	Old Rose (944)	Old Rose (944) 50% + Sunny Skintone (845) 50%		
Hair & moustache	Black (950)	Chocolate Brown (872)		
Grey hairs	Neutral Grey (992) 50% + Black (950) 50%	Neutral Grey (992)		
Weapons' wood	Hull Red (985)	Hull Red (985) 50% + Mahogany Brown (846) 50%	Mahogany Brown (846)	
Iron	Chainmail (61-56) 80% + Black (950) 20%	Chainmail (61-56)		
Brass	Shining Gold (61-63) 80% + Black (950) 20%	Shining Gold (61-63)		
Trousers' reinforcements	Black (950)	Black (950) 90% + Raw Sienna (113) 10%	1st highlight 90% + Raw Sienna (113) 10%	
Sabretache	Black (950)	Black (950) 90% + Neutral Grey (992) 10%	1st highlight 90% + Neutral Grey (992) 10%	
Colback	Black (950)	Black (950) 80% + Neutral Grey (992) 20% *db*	1st highlight 80% + Neutral Grey (992) 20% *db*	

HORSE

There aren't many differences from the painting process explained in the chapter devoted to horses, besides reducing the contrast between the highlights.

1. Over the white priming we'll apply the undercoat (Figure 347) and, once dry, three consecutive highlights (Figures 348-350).

(Figure 348)

(Figure 347)

(Figure 350)

(Figure 349)

(Figure 351)

(Figure 352)

2. Once the horse's coat is finished, we'll paint the base colours of the black points (to make a bay), white marks, as well as the hooves, the eyes, the teeth (Figure 351) and the belts and reins. Finally, we'll give two highlights to all these colours (Figures 352-353) except to the eyes, where just a touch of white is needed, and the reins, which will be highlighted later.

3. Once the horse is painted, we'll do the equipment (Figure 354), starting by the shabraque. Here we'll use the drybrush technique so, as noted before, it's recommended to do it sooner rather than later. Once this is done, line everything on it with black and paint all the remaining areas (Figure 355).

(Figure 3

(Figure 354)

(Figure 355)

209

Bay horse	Base colour	1st highlight	2nd highlight	3rd highlight
Coat	Mahogany Brown (846) 70% + Black (950) 30%	Base colour 80% + Mahogany Brown (846) 20%	1st highlight 80% + Mahogany Brown (846) 20%	2nd highlight 80% + Tan Yellow (912) 20%
Points	Black (950)	Black (950) 90% + Raw Sienna (113) 10%	1st highlight 90% + Raw Sienna (113) 10%	
Tail & mane	Black (950)	Black (950) 80% + Neutral Grey 20% (992) db	1st highlight 80% + Neutral Grey (992) 20% db	
Marks	Light Grey (990)	Light Grey (990) 50% + White (951) 50%	1st highlight 10% + White (951) 90%	
Teeth	Raw Sienna (113)	Raw Sienna (113) 50% + Tan Yellow (912) 50%	Tan Yellow (912)	
Hooves	Beige Brown (875)	Beige Brown (875) 50% + Tan Yellow (912) 50%	1st highlight 10% + Tan Yellow (912) 90%	
Reins & pistol holders	Black (950)	Black (950) 90% + Neutral Grey (992) 10%	1st highlight 90% + Neutral Grey (992) 10%	
Belts	Sky Grey (989)	Sky Grey (989) 50% + White (951) 50%	White (951)	
Sheepskin	Light Grey (990) 50% + Raw Sienna (113) 50%	White (951) db		
Sheepskin (inside)	Beige Brown (875)	Beige Brown (875) 70% + Tan Yellow (912) 30%	1st highlight 70% + Tan Yellow (912) 30%	
Shabraque's wolfteeth	Cavalry Brown (982)	Cavalry Brown (982) 50% + Red (947) 50%	Red (947) 90% + Scarlet (817) 10%	
Valise	Prussian Blue (965) 70% + Black (950) 30%	Base Colour 10% + Prussian Blue (965) 90%	1st highlight 90% + White (951) 10%	
Valise piping	Raw Sienna (113)	Yellow Ochre (913)		
Saddle	Hull Red (985)	Hull Red (985) 50% + Mahogany Brown (846) 50%	Mahogany Brown (846)	
Blanket	Chocolate Brown (872)	Chocolate Brown (872) 90% + White (951) 10%	1st highlight 90% + White (951) 10%	
Iron	Chainmail (61-56) 80% + Black (950) 20%	Chainmail (61-56)		
Brass	Shining Gold (61-63) 80% + Black (950) 20%	Shining Gold (61-63)		

21

Smaller Scales

Although 28mm became the queen of wargame figure sizes, there is life beyond it, especially outside of the UK. In countries such as Spain and Italy, 15/18mm is more popular. Although less spectacular than 28mm, 15/18mm has some intrinsic advantages: it requires less space to store, gaming tables need not be huge and it's cheaper and easier to paint. On the other hand, other sizes, such as 6mm or 10mm are growing in popularity. I especially like 10mm, as these figures can be painted quite easily and fast but still have a good amount of detail.

WWII Red Army Cossacks, Battlefield Miniatures, 20 mm.

Using the 28mm painting methods shown in this book for smaller scales is not impossible but in my opinion it is a waste of time. These are wargame figures where the numbers in each unit, rather than the quality of painting, makes the difference. I'm not suggesting ignoring these figures at all, but I suggest finding a good balance between quality and the time spent on every figure. We are talking about building armies, not lavishing attention on a single miniature such as the 40mm hussar shown in the previous chapter.

Thus, we'll simplify our standard painting system to adapt it to the scale of the miniature being painted. As a general rule the smaller the miniature the simpler and faster the painting.

20MM

This classic size, equivalent (and mainly compatible) to 1/72 or 1/76 plastic figures and model kits, is very popular, especially amongst Second World War wargamers. Roughly halfway between 28mm and 15mm, I paint them exactly like 28mm figures (base colour plus two

(Figure 356)

(Figure 357)

highlights). However, faster painting methods could be used, closer to those described below for the 15/18 mm.

15/18MM

This is the perfect wargame figure size for many people, and was also the size of my first historical miniatures (Essex Napoleonic Russians), so I'm quite fond of it. Despite the smaller size, you can make an exquisite job of painting 15/18mm figures, exactly like a 28mm miniature, but as the point is to build units and then armies, there really is no need to spend so much time with every single miniature.

Starting with the undercoat, use a white primer if you are to use patinas, or black otherwise. The base colours will be painted as usual. The main difference from 28mm is the number of highlights, using just one as a general rule and two for horses. On the other hand, the contrast should be higher. The 28mm colour charts could be easily adapted for 15/18mm using the same base colours mentioned there but skipping the first highlight and just using the second highlight instead.

Black undercoat

For this step-by-step we are using a metal Napoleonic French fusilier from the Spanish company Xan Miniatures (Figures 356-357). As usual, it was glued in an empty bottle and then primed in black.

1. First of all we'll paint the base colours of the predominant parts of the uniform: Prussian Blue (965) plus Black (950) for the coat, Sky Grey (989) for the lapels, waistcoat and turnbacks and Sky Grey (989) plus Raw Sienna (113) for the off-white trousers (Figure 358). Next we'll paint one highlight on all these areas with Prussian Blue (965), White (951) and the trousers base colour plus White (951) respectively (Figure 359).

2. Now it's time for the secondary parts of the uniform.

(Figure 358)

(Figure 359)

(Figure 360)

(Figure 361)

The base colours will be Cavalry Brown (982) for collar and cuffs, Beige Brown (875) for face and hands and Chocolate Brown (872) for the knapsack and the blanket (Figures 360-361). On highlights, we'll use Red (947) for collar and cuffs, Flat Flesh (955) for the face and hands, Beige Brown (875) for the knapsack and Chocolate Brown (872) plus White (951) for the blanket. The face could be plainer, but I decided to recreate a miniature version of myself and gave it a five o'clock shadow and a rosy lower lip (Figures 362-363). At this stage we'll paint the collar, cuffs, lapels and turnbacks piping.

3. With the major parts already painted, now it's time to add minor details such as shako, musket and belts.

(Figure 362)

(Figure 363)

213

French fusilier	Base colour	1st highlight
Coat & fatigue cap	Prussian Blue (965) 80% + Black (950) 20%	Prussian Blue (965)
Lapels, waistcoat & turnbacks	Sky Grey (989)	White (951)
Trousers	Sky Grey (989) 50% + Raw Sienna (113) 50%	Base colour 50% + White (951) 50%
Collar & cuffs	Cavalry Brown (982)	Red (947)
Red piping		Red (947)
White piping		White (951)
Face & hands	Beige Brown (875)	Flat Flesh (955)
Five o'clock shadow	Beige Brown (875)	Beige Brown (875) 50% + White (951) 50%
Lower lip		Old Rose (944)
Knapsack	Chocolate Brown (872)	Beige Brown (875)
Blanket	Chocolate Brown (872)	Chocolate Brown (872) 60% + White (951) 40%
Shako & cartridge box	Black (950)	Black (950) 70% + White (951) 30%
Shako cords	Light Grey (990)	White (951)
Shako pompom	Prussian Blue (965)	Prussian Blue (965) + White (951)
Shoes	Black (950)	Black (950) + Raw Sienna (113)
Musket & bayonet scabbard	Hull Red (985)	Mahogany Brown (846)
Belts	Buff (976) White (951)	
Iron		Chain Mail (61-56)
Brass		Shining Gold (61-63)

General Zayas's Division in the Battle of the Albuera (1811). From left to right: 2nd and 4th Royal Spanish Guards, Walloon Guards, Patria, Toledo and Legión Extranjera. In the rear, Irlanda and Ciudad Real. Warmodelling Miniatures, 18 mm.

The use of patinas for 15/18mm is strongly recommended for both a fast and a quality paint job. As we have seen before, the main difference is the undercoat, white instead of black, and the painting process. Instead of painting the base colours and highlights progressively, as we have done with the French fusilier, the steps to follow will be:

1. All base colours

2. Patina

3. First highlight

4. Second highlight (optional, just for horses, elephants and so on)

The same considerations regarding contrast and 28mm colour charts are still valid, but bear in mind that the use of a patina will increase the degree of contrast. So, if you like a regular contrast, use the colour combination stated in the charts for the first highlight, but if you prefer extra contrast, like this Essex Carthaginian elephant (Figure 364), go straight for the second highlight ignoring the first.

(Figure 364)

(Figure 365)

(Figure 366)

(Figure 367)

10/6MM

The advantages of 6mm and 10mm are obvious: even cheaper than 15/18mm, faster to paint and less demanding on storage and gaming space. I use three different techniques to deal with these tiny miniatures.

Black undercoat: high-quality finish

This painting process is similar to the 15mm one, but eliminating the second highlight for horses. Let's use Pendraken's General Lee as an example:

1. First of all, we'll glue the miniature to an empty bottle and prime it black (Figure 365).

2. We'll then paint the base colours, as shown in the 28mm colour charts (Figure 366).

3. Finally, paint a highlight using the colour combination shown in the 28mm colour charts for the second highlight (Figure 367), or the third highlight for horses. As you can see, some parts such as the boots and the reins have no highlight added.

General Lee	Base colour	1st highlight
Coat	Neutral Grey (992) 80% + Black (950) 20%	Neutral Grey (992)
Saddle cloth	Grey Blue (949) 80% + Black (950) 20%	Grey Blue (949)
Face	Beige Brown (875) Flat Flesh (955)	
Gloves	Raw Sienna (113)	Buff (976)
Hat	Beige Brown (875)	Tan Yellow (912)
Hair & beard	Light Grey (990)	White (951)
Horse's coat	Light Grey (990)	White (951)
Mane, tail & points	Black (950)	Black (950) 70% + Neutral Grey (992) 30%
Boots & reins	Black (950)	
Metal spurs & bite		Chain Mail (61-56)

Black undercoat: fast painting

Although the previous method looks good, especially given the size of the miniature, in my opinion is very time consuming, and painting these smaller figures should be as quick as possible. So a good alternative (and how I paint my own 10mm armies) is to use the black base both as the undercoat and the base colours, just painting one highlight over the black. Admittedly this looks odd when you see the

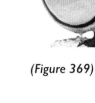

(Figure 369)

Pendraken Greek in the photo (Figures 368-369), but remember that the figure is very magnified in the photo as is only 10mm tall in real life! Complete units painted in this way look great when they're on the tabletop (Figure 370).

igure 368)

(Figure 370)

Patinas

This is the quickest way to paint smaller scales, and achieves very good results. The method is similar to that for 15/18mm figures but without the highlights. The step-by-step process for this Pendraken Carthaginian elephant was:

1. Assemble the different parts of the figure and glue it to an empty bottle. Prime it white (Figure 371).

2. Paint all the base colours (Figure 372), but use the lighter colour recommended on the 28mm chart for the first or second highlight rather than the base colour.

3. Apply the patina. As we're not painting a highlight, don't use a dark shade: a medium or light shade looks a lot better, and that's what I did with the elephant (Figure 373). A darker shade would make the figure look too dark on the table.

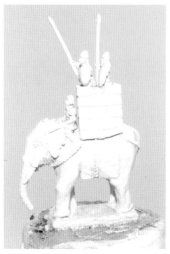

(Figure 371)

(Figure 372)

(Figure 373)

Carthaginian elephant	Base colour
Elephant	Neutral Grey (992) 50% + Beige Brown (875) 50%
Tower	Raw Sienna (113)
Blanket	Blue Grey (943)
Ropes	Tan Yellow (912)
Mahout's skin	Beige Brown (875)
Mahout's cloth	Tan Yellow (912)
Spearmen's skin	Flat Flesh (955)
Spearmen's linen armour	White (951)
Spearmen's metal armour	Brass (801)
Spearman 1's tunic	Red (947)
Spearman 2's tunic	Blue Grey (943)
Spear shafts	Mahogany Brown (846)
Spear points	Chainmail (61-56)